Effective Defense

D0920468

The Woman,
The Plan,
The Gun

by Gila May-Hayes
foreword by Massad F. Ayoob

About the cover:
Self-defense tools are effective only if they are in your possession when the attack occurs. Resting on DeSantis' compact holster bag, "The Executive" (Patents #4966320 and 5170919), is Smith & Wesson's 3913, a 9mm semi-automatic handgun that is very light, compact and easy to conceal. The author recommends carrying a can of oleoresin capcisum aerosol to deter less-than-lethal assailants. Carried on the keyring, a Monadnock Persuader is useful in defense against grabbing and other contact attacks.

Published in the United States of America by The Firearms Academy of Seattle, Inc., P.O. Box 2814, Kirkland, WA 98083.
                         Printed in the U.S.A.

ISBN 1-885036-01-9

Table of Contents

Foreword

It was an honor to be asked to do the foreword for Gila May-Hayes' first book. I originally met Gila in the early 90s when she attended one of my courses sponsored in Seattle by her then-instructor and future husband, Marty Hayes. It was a large class, but Gila's intensity and incisive questioning would have made her stand out to any instructor.

In the years since, Gila has taken several courses with me, and with many of the other instructors I most respect: John Farnam, Jim Cirillo, Marty Hayes, Jim Lindell, Ed Nowicki and Greg Hamilton among others. She has absorbed their training and made it work.

Gila's book contains a good deal of the material I teach at Lethal Force Institute. Sometimes it's best to see a technique or a concept through the eye of the student instead of from the instructor's perspective: often, your own needs are closer to those of the student than those of the instructor, so the student's perspective serves you better.

The author of this book can do what she teaches, make no mistake about that. I've shot with her in matches that range from local events to world class shoots, and she's always held up her end admirably, generally firing powerful +P loads from a .45 automatic using the intense Isosceles stance you'll see in the photos. She's damn good at it, too. When I'm shooting for money, I don't allow second-raters on my team.

I've seen Gila take a man literally twice her size down to his knees grimacing in agony with a Number Two Kubaton wrist lock. In weapon retention training, I've seen her allow such a monster to get a good, strong hold on her dummy gun with both hands...before she executed the techniques and literally threw him away. It's a pleasure to watch her do this. Even more satisfying than the impact when the "attacker" hits the ground is the expression of absolute disbelief on his face.

In short, Gila May-Hayes is living proof that a woman doesn't need to be Tugboat Annie, Mrs. Doubtfire, or the Amazon Queen to hold her own in a fight with a much larger and very aggressive male attacker. If such a man should ever attack the author of this book, he'll have written his own cause of death for the autopsy report: "Sudden and acute failure of the victim selection process."

You'll probably be able to tell from the pictures that Gila is a petite, slender, very attractive and very feminine women. She now takes her rightful position in the ranks of others in the "women and guns" movement—Sonny Jones, Paxton Quigley, Graciella Casillas, Elizabeth Swayze, Barbara Budnar, and Dr. Lyn Bates, to name a few—as role models who prove that femininity does not have to be compromised or sacrificed to achieve strength and self-reliance.

I enjoyed reading the draft manuscript of the book you now hold in your hands. It means a lot to me that Gila was able to absorb so much of what I offered her. At the end of each class, I remind the students that they have an almost sacred duty to share this knowledge with other good people who have need of it. I'm very proud of Gila: she has done this, far more than most.

I will share Gila's book with my daughters, and with my wife, and with my female students. I will do so for the same reason that I hope you, too, will share it with others once you've absorbed it.

This is the kind of book that can save a woman's life.

> — Massad Ayoob
> Director, Lethal Force Institute
> Concord, New Hampshire, USA
> January, 1994

Introduction

Like lots of women, my only contact with firearms were the rifles and shotguns my dad kept, unloaded, behind the back door. He used the guns on a limited basis to control varmints on our Wyoming ranch. Although I'd watch him leave the house with a .22 rifle, I never saw him shoot the gun, nor was I ever given the opportunity to handle the rifles. I understood they were off limits, and left them strictly alone. I didn't think much about firearms until I was in my 30s, divorced and back in college, when my employer transferred me to a swing shift. My car was old and my apartment was in a risky neighborhood not far from downtown Seattle.

I assured my personal safety by simply not leaving my apartment after dark, and carrying a can of oleoresin capsicum spray and a heavy chain. The assignment to swing shift changed everything. Commuting down Seattle's Interstate 5 at 2 a.m. required a better defense than any I could muster. I had completed just enough karaté and women's self defense to know I could not hold off an attacker much larger than I.

As my new shift assignment neared, I worried a lot about personal safety. The answer came unexpectedly in a professor's college dissertation that discussed the reasons people gave when applying for permits to carry a concealed weapon. Ah, ha! I exclaimed. Of course! I need a gun!

Going to unfamiliar places was difficult for me. I was timid and hated not knowing what questions to ask. I didn't know what *caliber* meant, much less what to look for in a handgun. Looking back, I'm not sure I even knew the difference between a revolver and a semi-automatic. After visiting several gun and pawn shops, I knew that simply holding or looking at the guns would not answer my questions. There were big revolvers, little revolvers, and mysterious semi-automatics. I couldn't get the answers—let alone articulate the questions—to intelligently select my first gun.

On the recommendation of a sporting goods clerk, I went to an indoor gun range and rented four or five guns. I favored the simpler revolvers, and after several hours of shooting, decided on a .38 snub nosed revolver. It proved an excellent gun for concealed carry. While I seldom carry the little revolver anymore, it is a good gun—completely reliable and small enough to carry anywhere.

After several visits to the range, I realized I couldn't teach myself to shoot. I also knew that although I had applied for a permit to carry a concealed weapon, I had little understanding of my state's gun laws. Fortunately, one of the shooting instructors I contacted had written a book on local gun laws, and that introduction led me into a progressive course of training. I spent most of my spare time and money the next year going through the instructor's entire curriculum—studies ranging from an afternoon handgun safety seminar through high-stress tactical exercises at The Firearms Academy of Seattle's highest level of training.

I learned grip, shooting stances, trigger control, sight picture and follow through—all the basics of shooting. The courses introduced me to Massad Ayoob, and I completed Levels I and II of Lethal Force Institute training. I took John Farnam's defensive handgun course, three days of instruction and shooting drills using steel plate targets. A practice of continuing study with various instructors had started.

I was accepted in a firearms instructor program, concentrating on teaching beginning women's classes as my first year of gun ownership drew to a close. A few months later I was certified to teach, and now continue to teach the principles of shooting and use of deadly force. I later completed Washington State Criminal Justice Commission's 40-hour firearms instructor certification course for armed security officers, presented by Bill Burris and Phil Shave.

Since then I've concentrated on teaching basic shooting skills and writing for the firearms media. Sonny Jones, then-editor of *Women & Guns*, gave me my first assignment, reviewing handguns as a monthly feature for the magazine. The association continued when Peggy Tartaro stepped in as editor, and with her acceptance, I began to write a monthly training column, "Personal Trainer," in addition to the gun reviews. Both assignments gave me an unequalled opportunity to get hands-on experience with guns and gear that would have been impossible to buy and examine as a consumer.

At every opportunity, I enroll in firearms classes from top instructors Massad Ayoob, John Farnam, Jim Cirillo and others. As an instructor, I've earned certification through the National Law Enforcement Training Center to teach Weapon Retention and CAS Expandable Baton as well as instructor certification from Ed Nowicki of R.E.B. Security Training to teach oleoresin capsicum spray defense. I've become a strong believer in strong tactics and intermediate defenses to fend off a harasser *before* the confrontation turns lethal or to "buy" enough time to draw a weapon after a surprise attack. I have a continuing interest in the martial arts because they create awareness and hone speed and responsiveness. I urge women to learn to use the Monadnock Persuader or Kubotan as an intermediate weapon they can carry at all times.

As you read the pages that follow, please understand that the advice, the thoughts, and the concepts are distilled and gathered from many sources in the firearms and self defense field. Personal gratitude goes to Massad Ayoob, my husband Marty Hayes, John Farnam, Vicki Farnam, Jim Cirillo, and Evan Marshall. They are my friends and my teachers. A thank-you back through time to De Gassaway, who made karaté fun. And a thank-you to the students who touch me and let me touch their lives. I learn from each one who comes through a class.

There is little original thought involved in this kind of work; it involves synthesizing the best information available and presenting it to women who have decided to take responsibility for their survival. Consider me a conduit, passing along information that has worked for me and for other women.

Finally, the completion of this book would not have been possible without the generous help of many friends. I don't know how to give sufficient thanks to all of them. Massad Ayoob has taught and inspired me. He is the master in my lineage, one who has synthesized material from many sources into one cohesive, life-saving discipline. His generous agreement to review the manuscript and write the foreword for

Effective Defense is invaluable. Personal friends have given enormous time and support. Friend and colleague Norm Aubin gave *hours* of darkroom time, printing pictures for illustrations. Editor Susie Hampton-Streng pruned my sometimes muddled verbiage and organized my thoughts into coherent sentences. John Barnett at the Second Amendment Foundation gave encouragement and publishing advice. Richard Morgan, Kendra Aubin, DeAnne Orive, "Fuzzy" Fletcher, Norm Aubin, Marty Hayes, Marlys May, Brady Wright, Terry Hollis, Karl Wingren, Phil Steinert, Clinton Hansen and others played roles for illustrative pictures. My husband, Marty, has been a guiding force through my development as an instructor. He has introduced me to some of the nation's leading instructors, taken me to major competitions years before I would have considered competing, and pushed me to always achieve a higher level of shooting skill. He originally conceived this book, and has been present through it all, reading, suggesting, taking photos and lending invaluable support.

Gila May-Hayes
Kirkland, Washington
1994

1
Women's Rights and Responsibilities

I grew up with my mother's repertoire of fears: attack by strangers, rape, and other violent acts by men against women. She warned me to avoid strangers, to keep window shades down, but never in the "training" was there any mention of self defense. Dress modestly and bad men will not bother you, I was told. Common sense measures, like lowering window shades before undressing, are good and necessary, but what could we do if someone attacked even the most careful, modest woman? The training was in avoidance; we had no game plan if evasion failed. Girls weren't allowed to fight, even in self defense. We feared violence but weren't allowed to respond in kind.

A lot of things have changed. We now know that rape and assault can happen to *anyone*, anywhere. I have come to believe we are responsible for our own survival. Just as a woman exercises and eats wholesome food, she needs to prepare herself for the eventuality that she may be among the 75% of American women who face violent assault, rape, or murder in their life time.[1] In 1992 Surgeon General Antonio Novello stated that the leading cause of injuries to women between the ages of 15 to 44 was physical violence.[2]

Senator Joseph Biden headed a committee that found at least 1.1 million women were victims of assault, aggravated assault, murder, or rape reported to police in 1991. Noting that a vast number of rapes and assaults go unreported, the Biden committee estimated that three to four times the number of reported assaults occurred.[3]

In a world where women are responsible for earning their own living (and often are sole support of their children), it is ironic that women have not become wholly responsible for their own self defense. Women who had or longed for strong fathers often feel there should always be a "daddy" nearby to fend off violent assailants. Some transfer that responsibility to God, law enforcement officers, husbands, lovers, or friends. We spend much of our time alone, in situations where no one is near enough to respond in time to stop an assault. Each woman must be capable of her own self defense.

Gun control proponents have argued that Americans should give up their armaments and rely on the police to protect them. Realistically, however, police forces are installed to patrol, maintain peace, and *investigate crimes after the fact*, not prevent the crimes. In 1975, three women were raped, sodomized, and terrorized for fourteen hours in Washington, D.C. The police were called in the initial moments of the attack, and four cruisers were dispatched. None of the victims was able to answer the door, and after five minutes the officers left. A second call received a promise of help on the way. It was later determined that officers were never dispatched to answer the second plea for help. Fortunately, the women survived. Lawsuits followed, and in 1981 the Court of Appeals for Washington, D.C., ruling on Warren v. District of Columbia, wrote that under American law the "government and its agents are under no general duty to provide public services, such as police protection, to any individual citizen."[4]

Citing *Warren vs. District of Columbia* is in no way an indictment or harsh judgment of police officers. The men and women who work in law enforcement put their lives on the line every time they start their shift. As civilians, we need to recognize that their function cannot be our moment-to-moment protection. The role of protector ultimately rests with the individual.

To be female is to be a life-giver. We should expand our role to be life-preservers, as well. That means, after deliberation and training, developing the ability and willingness to take life from any who would take our life or harm those in our care. When women can't defend themselves, a society that perceives, trains, and treats women as victims and less equal members is created and perpetrated. The abuse will be acted out by strangers, by acquaintances, or by mates. When women are viewed as meek, defenseless prey, all women— from the bravest to the most timid—are subject to victimization.

If there was a magic bullet, the perfect weapon for a woman, or any other "perfect" mode of feminine self defense, it would be worthless without the woman's determination to preserve her life and well-being *at the expense, if necessary, of her assailant's life.*

The well-meaning woman who buys a gun, saying that she plans to just threaten an assailant, doesn't understand the mind of the victimizer. How can a serial rapist face the specter of being returned to the penitentiary where, when asked how he landed back in jail, he will have to relate that a woman threatened him with a little .38? Think about it! His response will likely be a challenge: "Go ahead and shoot me, bitch!" He knows instinctively that his victim is mentally unprepared to defend herself and he implicitly believes our society's standard that women give life, not take it away. Pray to God that more rapists encounter women who have broken this societal norm.

Men who victimize women act out of hatred for women, and do so in pursuit of power and domination more than sexual gratification. When women have matured to the extent that they are willing to spill the blood of an assailant before sacrificing their own lives, I believe we will find fewer men who are willing to risk injury or death to rape and kill.

A survey published in 1986 showed that over a third of felons questioned said they worried about being shot by their intended victim, and over half agreed that "most criminals are more worried about meeting an armed victim than they are about running into the police."[5]

In a period of 11 months, two armed Seattle women, one using a .22, stopped rapists. A small caliber gun shot wound rarely brings an instant stop, and did not in this case. It did, however, convince the rapist to break off the attack. The man shot with the .22 ran into the hallway where he died minutes later, the second rapist dodged four bullets and cowered in the bathroom until police arrived.

My fantasy of a perfect world is one where he who assaults, terrorizes, or takes advantage of a woman challenges an individual of equal defensive ability. How can this fantasy come true, when the female gender is physically smaller than the male? Disparity of force is ultimately balanced by mindset—the determination to defend one's life—and by training and acquisition of the appropriate tools to support that determination.

Until we accept that power and responsibility, we continue to *fuel* the abuse that takes the peace and safety from our lives.

[1] *Violence Against Women: A Week in the Life of America*, a majority staff report prepared for the Committee on the Judiciary, United States Senate, 102nd Congress, 2nd Session, October 1992.

[2] *Journal of the American Medical Association*, Vol. 267, No. 23, p. 3132, June 17, 1992.

[3] *Violence Against Women: A Week in the Life of America*.

[4] Senate Judiciary Committee, Majority Staff, July 31, 1990.

[5] Wright, J. & Rossi, P., *Armed and Considered Dangerous: A Survey of Felons and their Firearms* (1986), published by Aldine de Guyter Press; based on data from a survey formerly released by the National Institute of Justice.

2
The Will to Survive

Women's responses to using deadly force in self defense range from absurd to frightening to savvy.

"I want a gun so I can point it at a rapist to scare him away."

"There's no reason to practice with my gun—I only keep it by the bed in case someone breaks into the house."

"I won't carry a gun because I'm not sure I could kill someone." (Better.)

"I feel my life-style puts me at risk, so I need a gun and I need to know how and when to use it." (Yes!)

The doubt that asked "Can I kill to preserve my own life?" finally left my mind after an immersion in the doctrine of justifiable use of deadly force. I suggest similar studies for women plagued with questions about of their ability to kill in self defense. Read and reread Massad Ayoob's *In the Gravest Extreme*; attend his seminars if possible.

My mental determination started with firearms training that included videotaped lectures by Massad Ayoob, an authority on the rightful use of deadly force. His frank discussions of the danger, illustrated by case histories and their adjudication in American courts, confirmed my belief that I was at risk and strengthened my desire to protect myself. Ayoob's two-day Use of Deadly Force seminar was an emotional challenge. The material forced me to confront a fear of attack that has been with me since earliest childhood. At the end of two days, I started to believe it was my right to stop a threat to my life. I left the seminar drained, but empowered and a little euphoric, as I experienced for the first time my own right to survival.

I still find it hard to listen to story after story of victimization and assault, but my immersion in this study of self defense has burned away much of the emotional baggage of feeling powerless. Gone is the part that *believed* that being female meant being a powerless victim.

Deciding to live

The will to fight won't just come to you as you face an assailant. If you have not answered questions about your right to defend yourself, those same questions will be foremost in your mind, interfering with the thoughts that *should* be directing your defensive tactics. I don't think an ethical person can simply say "Sure, I believe that it's OK to kill to save my own life," without understanding what it means to kill in self defense. Read the work of Ayoob, John Farnam, and Paxton Quigley.[1] Study the stories of those who have been forced to kill in self defense and what they have experienced in the aftermath. You need to understand the implications, accept the responsibility, and decide to fight back.

I don't think you can discuss the self defense mindset without discussing the moral aspect of use of deadly force. Every ethical woman who takes up self defense should ask herself, "is it right for me to take a life to save my own?" Interestingly, the question is easier to answer affirmatively when phrased, "Is it right for me to kill to protect the lives of my children or my geriatric parents?" Now consider the following query: "Is it right to take the life of an assailant who would kill me, orphan my children, and widow my spouse?"

The primary concept in the self defense mindset is:

> *The assailant forfeited his right to live when he began the assault with intent to kill or cripple.*

Even Christianity, with its doctrine of putting others first, only requires that you lay down your life for a friend—not for a deranged predator who would take not only *your* life, but would take the lives of others after leaving you or your survivors to deal with the aftermath of his behavior. How different recent history could have been if Kenneth Bianchi, Ted Bundy, or other serial killers had met with an armed woman who put her survival first!

Your decision to fight back grows stronger when you understand the conditions under which the law and society condones use of deadly force. Killing in defense of property will reap a grave punishment. And though killing in self defense will also earn societal disapproval, clear-cut cases of self defense are court-defensible and the survivor can deal with the fallout, alive to do so.

A serious study of use of deadly force results in a mature conviction to use this ultimate power only to preserve innocent life, not to bully or threaten. *The Decision* is one that places ultimate value on innocent human life, not pride or material possessions. Prepare yourself and make the decision to survive. Make it with love for yourself, for your family and for your gender and society. This is not a decision to become a cold-blooded killer; this is a decision to honor and preserve that spark of life that is *you*.

Inoculation

As you internalize *The Decision*, you may find yourself dealing with dreams and day-time fantasies about assault and self defense—with varying results. Ayoob calls it the inoculation process, and most experience it as we begin to absorb concepts of self defense and rightful use of lethal force. It seems to be the mind's way of dealing with concepts that run counter to our earliest training to "turn the other cheek." The dreams are your social conscience's way of questioning the *rightness* of your newly-embraced determination to survive. The best advice I can give is to accept it, don't judge yourself harshly for your thoughts; understand that your mind is weighing the unfair constraints society has imposed on women, against your new belief that you have the right to survive unmolested.

A student told me that although she made it through her first months of carrying a gun without the nightmares, she felt guilty because she thoroughly enjoyed shooting her gun. It seemed terrible to *like* something capable of deadly results, she said. Like all of us, she needed the company of like-minded individuals who could share similar experiences and confirm that she had not become evil. Other students have reported feelings of anxiety, as they grapple with the concept of using deadly force in self defense. Women often report that their friends are appalled by their interest in guns.

You may find it difficult to discuss your growing belief that you have the right to employ deadly force to stop a lethal assault. There is a limited pool of people who share this conviction—parents, co-workers and friends may not be able to respond supportively to the feelings you need to discuss. As civilians, and even more as women, we belong to a limited peer group who will take the steps necessary to prevent rape, murder or violent assault. Our support group is extremely limited. Beyond the practical aspect of good training, classes can provide contact with like-minded people—and a class that meets *your* needs will likely contain other women who are dealing with the same concerns. Women's self defense groups, as well as the women's division of the National Rifle Association can put you in touch with groups and instructors who share your concerns.[2]

At last, it is time for the good news: women are far less likely than men to be damned by society if they have to use the handgun to stop a rape or assault. Men are often burdened with the macho idea that they have to fight man-to-man. Society's portrayal of the helpless female corroborates her need to use deadly force against a rapist or murderer. As a result, the woman who has already decided to pull the trigger in self defense is more decisive if faced with an assailant who intends her harm. After the assault, she will suffer less condemnation from society and will answer fewer accusations that she used unnecessary force to save her life.

I am not going to regale you with tale after tale of rapes and assaults. I don't have the emotional fortitude to tell the stories. What I am going to tell you is when and why it is all right for you to fire your handgun to stop the threat to you or other innocent life.

---

[1] Ayoob's *In the Gravest Extreme*, Farnam's *The Street Smart Gun Book* and Quigley's *Armed and Female* are generally available in retail gun stores or can be ordered on the east coast from Police Bookshelf, (800) 624-9049 and from FAS Books on the west coast, (800) 327-2666.

[2] Arming Women Against Rape and Endangerment (AWARE), P.O. Box 242, Bedford, MA 01730-0242.

National Rifle Association of America, Women's Issues and Information, 1600 Rhode Island, Ave., N.W., Washington, D.C. 20036-3270.

American Women's Self Defense Association, 713 N. Wellwood Ave., Lindenhurst, NY 11757.

3
When May I Shoot?

I don't think very many first-time gun owners immediately realize the power they have assumed—and the resultant responsibility. I know long-time gun owners who talk like they haven't a clue about their responsibilities if the situation causes them to employ deadly force. I'm as uneasy with people who talk "big" and say things like "If anyone tries to break into my house, I'll shoot the *#@^ right through the door," as I am with someone who has a gun but isn't sure they can use it to stop a lethal assault.

When does the law allow me to use my gun in self defense? The question deals with issues of legality, morality and just plain common sense. The first issue, legality, will vary from state to state, and is subject to the mood of the prosecutors and judges currently serving in your area. There are some broad parameters that define justifiable use of lethal force, however, and I credit Massad Ayoob's excellent instruction and written material for the information that follows. Meeting Ayoob and listening to his lectures strengthened both my determination and my caution in matters of self defense. As we discuss the concepts of justifiable use of lethal force, I think you'll see the constant interplay of caution and courage.

American women are products of our society's Judeo-Christian conditioning and no one raised in our culture forms a conscience or social code without the influence of these values and ethics. Even non-believers, unless they are psychopathic, behave in accordance to these basic tenets. Out of this Judeo-Christian code we—and the society that judges our actions—form our response to use of lethal force. Both the legal and the moral codes have some foundation in plain old common sense. We will answer to the *reasonability* factor in deciding when to employ lethal force. "What would a reasonable and prudent person, under the same circumstances and knowing what you knew at the time, have done?" This yardstick is the concept of reasonableness as introduced by Ayoob in his lectures on judicious use of deadly force.

Most instructors who address lethal force teach three criteria required to justify using lethal force: *ability, opportunity* and *jeopardy*. The self defense shooter will need to prove that the person they killed had the *ability* to kill or cripple. This calls for presence of a deadly weapon, superiority in numbers, or the greater physical size and strength to cause death or crippling injury. Women and elderly people are at greater risk from unarmed assailants, since a larger person can over-power and kill or injure them without a weapon. In legalese, the concept that an unarmed but larger person can exert deadly force against a smaller person is called *disparity of force*. This concept has also been applied to women's societal conditioning, arguing that women are conditioned to submit and not to fight, putting them at greater risk from a determined, unarmed male assailant.

Did the assailant have the *opportunity* to harm you? You cannot shoot a person who yells a threat to strangle you from across a crowded street, because they cannot make good on the threat without closing the distance. Opportunity exists only when the threat can be acted on so rapidly that the intended victim cannot escape.

Finally, has the assailant put you in actual *jeopardy*? Verbal threats and

The frightening approach of dangerous-looking people is certainly cause for "preparation," but until intent to harm you has been clearly demonstrated, the gun must not be fired.

gestures do not justify killing unless the assailant's actions make it clear he intends to kill or cripple you *now*.

We will illustrate these concepts with a hypothetical situation, as it unfolds. Suppose your car failed as you were coming home from your 10-year old daughter's piano recital. The neighborhood you have to pass through to reach your home is one that harbors the city's most unfortunate and unsavory residents. You have gotten your car off the street and are wisely sitting inside, doors locked, waiting to signal a passing patrol car. Instead, you watch a pair of young men approach your car. One is carrying a length of heavy pipe. Your heart beat accelerates.

ABILITY

Do the men have the ability to cause grave bodily harm or death to you or another innocent person? Yes, two against one, or for that matter, one man against a woman is disparity of force; the pipe is an improvised street weapon. *Ability exists.*

As the men approach the car, you order your daughter to crouch between the front and back seats. You pull your revolver from your holster purse and hold it on your lap. "Get out! We're going to have some fun," orders one of the men. You respond with a forceful, "Go away, now!" but the passenger side window shatters under the impact of the pipe.

OPPORTUNITY

Is the threat close enough to inflict harm? A person cannot kill you from across the street, unless they wield a gun. Yes. When the car window was broken they came into range to kill or cripple you or your child. *Opportunity is present.*

You fling open your door, and fix the gun sights on the nearest assailant, ordering, "Don't move!" Instead, he sneers, "You'll never shoot me," and begins to come around the front of the car, brandishing the pipe.

JEOPARDY

Did the threat take specific action against you, causing you to believe he intended to cause crippling injury or death? Yes. When the pipe-wielder smashed your window and disregarded your command to stop, he put you in reasonable fear of death or crippling injury. *You are in jeopardy.*

21

Suppose, to continue this awful little tale, that the assailant rushes toward you and you pull the trigger. As the leader slumps across the hood of your car the other man turns and runs away. Can you shoot him in the back as he flees? No, no, no! No matter how terrifying the experience, you may only shoot *to stop the assault*. You must not shoot a fleeing felon who has clearly broken off the assault.

Do different rules apply inside the confines of your own home?

Suppose you hear noises in the basement during the daytime. Home alone, you take your loaded gun to check out the intrusion. This is no time to burst in, gun drawn with your finger on the trigger. You must know your target's identity before firing a panicked shot into a landlord, meter reader or other person authorized to be there.

Imagine a new scenario. You awake at 2 a.m. to hear movement in the dining room. You really should call 911, then gather all your dependents to one room and shoot only hostiles entering.

However, as you pause at the head of the stairs and see in the half-light a stranger holding a gun, you need not issue a challenge before opening fire. By breaking into your home armed, this criminal has forfeited all rights for a chance to rethink his position. A stranger with an exposed

Home defender aims the shotgun from behind cover, ensconced in a safe room.

gun is an *identifiable* threat. Don't give him the chance to fire on you first. You must take advantage of the element of surprise. He has the advantage of being physically well-awake and pumped up on adrenaline; his eyes are adjusted to the dark. His reflexes will likely exceed yours. Do not give the armed housebreaker a chance to shoot first. You may shoot without first issuing a challenge. Later, we will discuss tactical considerations in dealing with home intruders.

Unlike your duty to retreat if assailed on the street, there are few if any jurisdictions that require you to retreat from an invader in your own home. Evan Marshall, a well-recognized author in firearms and law-enforcement publications, now retired after 20 years with Detroit's police force, told me that during all his years in homicide, he never saw a citizen prosecuted for shooting a criminal in their house after a forced entry.

You must not fire at the criminal as he flees from your home. You may not shoot him as he is escaping. Some argue that you may kill a burglar as he escapes with your television or VCR, but that seems pretty uncivilized to me. Let him and your property go; the cost of that television is tiny compared to the legal fees you could incur defending yourself from civil lawsuit for crippling or killing this person.

Evan Marshall and the author enjoy a visit at the 1994 SHOT Show in Dallas, Texas.

Legal issues aside, there are a number of excellent reasons to earnestly avoid firing your weapon in self defense. They don't use the word aftermath for nothing.

One handed holstering lets you holster the gun without taking your eyes off the danger.

Post-shooting survival

If forced to shoot an assailant in self defense, you should be prepared for a number of events—dealing with the authorities, dealing with your internal responses, and dealing with a society that may not acknowledge the deadly danger that caused you to fire that shot.

To discuss dealing with the authorities, let's again draw up a hypothetical incident. You have just shot and stopped a knife-wielding criminal, who broke through your bedroom window screaming out his specific, evil intent. Joe Criminal falls and is no longer an immediate threat, so you order him into a controllable posture, prone, hands fully extended from sides, ankles crossed, his face turned away from you. This reduces the danger while you reload your weapon and call the police. Dial 911 and tell the dispatcher

- that an intruder is wounded and down at your address

- that you are holding him at gun point

- your physical description, to assure your correct identification by the responding officers

- the location of your safe room giving permission for the officers to break a door or window if necessary to gain entry.

You must be aware of two safety concerns:

Don't assume that your assailant can no longer harm you. Find a position behind furnishings that would stop him if he lunges for you, and always keep your gun pointed at the assailant.

You need to be able to get the gun out of sight when police officers arrive. The police have no choice but to consider *any* gun a threat. If your assailant is actively threatening, you need to keep the gun pointed at him, but be prepared to drop the gun on police orders when they enter the room. Be sure you maintain enough distance to drop the weapon out of your assailant's reach.

Be mentally prepared for the entry of the police officers. If they surprise you and you turn, gun in hand, to see who is coming in, there is a very good chance you will unintentionally point your gun toward the officers. This is convincingly threatening to merit shots from the police. Don't let a startled response cost your life.

Next you have to be concerned with giving the responding officers a balanced account of what occurred. You should not be uncooperative or secretive, but avoid giving confusing volumes of information.

Why not tell the cops everything? If you have just survived a look into death's abyss you will be eager to talk, make human contact, and eager to justify the horrible act you've just been forced to commit. The responding officer, who will file an official, court-admissible report is not the person with whom to share an emotional unburdening. Maintain emotional control—you can bare your soul to a religious advisor or private counselor later to excise the emotions. Priests and psychiatrist are generally exempt from court subpoena, so are safe resources for post-traumatic event therapy.

Reports from self defense shootings tell us that the perceptions of trauma survivors are very unreliable. A victim who makes a lengthy statement to the first officer through the door will probably relate incorrect information, especially about exact amounts of time, distances and other specifics.

During the stress of a violent encounter, the body and mind narrow their focus to the threat. This phenomenon, called the "tachypsychia" effect, causes tunnel vision, distortions in perceptions of time and space, degradation of fine motor skills, general muscle tightening, and tremors. In addition, hearing shuts down to only that which the mind determines is necessary for survival. Called auditory exclusion, this part of the phenomenon causes survivors to report that they never heard the shots they fired. It is a documented part of the human survival system, but one that can cause unnecessary trouble in court-admissible statements to police. The victim-survivor who must defend self defense actions in court needs expert witnesses who can educate the judge and jury about the body's reactions, including sensory exclusion, during a violent encounter. With documented studies in hand, the courts will be better able to understand and justify your act of self defense.

When law enforcement officers arrive on the scene of a self defense shooting, it is best to answer only general questions to avoid giving inaccurate information. If questioned extensively at the scene, it is appropriate to tell the investigating officer: "He assaulted me. I was forced to shoot before he killed or crippled us. You know how serious this is. I think I should call my attorney now."

Evan Marshall told me, "Cops hate to be told 'no,' but it is better for you to spend the night in lock-up than 20 years in the penitentiary because of information you gave right after a shooting."

After a police officer shoots someone, the officer is usually sequestered, away from the press and other information seekers, to let them settle their minds and emotions before making a statement or answering questions. You deserve the same consideration.

Have a well-thought out plan. If you ever face this situation, when asked what happened, tell the responding officers, "He assaulted me (or my child). I was forced to shoot to save my (my child's) life." Ayoob calls this style of reporting "the active dynamic." It truthfully describes what occurred and how it came about. Weigh the strength of a response that places your assailant in the aggressive, active role against: "I shot him twice after he came through the bedroom door." Both statements are true: the first gives a more accurate picture of the cause of the shooting. You had to shoot in response to his assault. It places responsibility for the outcome squarely on he who initiated the confrontation.

Marshall suggests admitting that you really wanted to run away. He advises this kind of report: "My first thought was to escape, but that wasn't possible. I yelled at him to leave, and when he came up the stairs toward me and my family, I had to fire in his direction."

Unless you are hospitalized as a result of the assault, you should expect to be taken to the police station after shooting in self defense. Women may be treated more gently than men, who may find themselves looking out through bars. You may be allowed only one phone call. Be sure you have laid the groundwork to make that one call productive. You should know, *in advance* your attorney's after-hours telephone number. This is no time for interference by an answering service paid *not* to disturb his attorneyship during the hours that most self defense situations transpire—dark of night or weekends.

Arrange in advance for a trusted associate or friend to contact attorneys and investigators. Explain that you want to prepare for the chance you might someday need to defend yourself. Ask if they would be willing to help in such a situation, explaining your understanding of the events that may follow a self defense shooting. If they agree, it is their number you memorize, and to them you direct your emergency call.

This trusted associate accepts the responsibility to contact your attorney if you are jailed. They should be given the attorney's office and off-hours telephone numbers, as well as those of close family members you might want told of your situation.

Your gun, and probably any other firearms in your home, will probably be taken away by investigating officers. The police have no way of immediately guaranteeing that you are innocent, so they will likely remove any guns until you are cleared of suspicion. The gun will be held as evidence until it is clear if any charges will be filed.

Now, if you have shot a gang member or someone with a vindictive, grief-crazed family member, this a terrible time to have lost your self defense tools. Once again, you can avoid this terror by advance planning. It is a good idea to obtain an affordable firearm and transfer its ownership to a trusted friend or relative, with the caveat that they will lend it to you at your request *no questions asked*.

And finally, remember that even if the authorities decide that there is no reason to charge you with a crime, you may be sued in civil court by the survivors of the person who assaulted you or sued by the assailant if he survives. As incomprehensible as it may seem, rapists' families surface, arguing that their "boy" could not have had a dark side. The jury will be faced with a puzzle: you appear before them alive, a survivor. It is difficult to perceive the survivor as a victim, too. They weigh your continuing life against the grief of the bereaved family. There is bound to be an element of sympathy for the dead person, in spite of atrocities they committed.

Attorney selection

The individual who has decided to use deadly force in self defense needs to have an attorney available, as we just discussed.

Evan Marshall recommends that individuals understand their own legal environment before they have to interact with the courts as a defendant. In small towns, the prosecutor often augments his or her salary with a private law practice. Marshall suggests making an appointment with the prosecutor, and spending an hour asking questions and getting advice about armed self defense and the mood of the court in such cases. "Get a receipt for the fee," Marshall advised. Not only does that prove that you seriously studied the legal ramifications of your self defense, but Marshall believes that the prosecutor will not be able to bring charges against someone that he or she has advised.

Another alternative Marshall suggests is to contact the lawyer who defends the police force after a shooting. This lawyer is valuable for his or her connections with the law enforcement community, Marshall said.

Finally, Marshall concludes, "know the lay of the land." Local politics and the personal beliefs and agendas of your local prosecutor can influence charges brought against someone who shoots in self defense. Ask the attorney you contact how courts in your area have treated self defense shootings.

Massad Ayoob emphasizes that citizens should not *retain* an attorney, nor should they seek out a famous criminal attorney. Keeping an attorney on retainer suggests that you expected to shoot someone. Famous criminal attorneys are remembered for "keeping bad guys out of jail," planting the suggestion that you are not innocent. Few criminal attorneys have the experience of defending innocent people, and may advise you to confess to a crime you did not commit, in exchange for a lenient sentence. A common tactic is pleading that the gun went off accidentally, instead of in an intentional act of self defense.

Ayoob suggests a relationship with an attorney who has retired from a judicial career. A retired judge is extremely well-connected and has an excellent grasp of current judicial attitudes.

Domestic abuse and acts of self defense

In *When Battered Women Kill,* author Angela Browne[1] cites a study group of 42 women, victims of domestic abuse and battering, who were charged in the death or serious injury of a husband or boyfriend. Of this group, about half were sentenced to jail terms, twelve received probation or suspended sentences, and only nine were acquitted. Jail sentences ranged from six months to 25 years, and one woman was sentenced to 50 years in prison. Browne quotes FBI statistics showing that fewer men are charged with first- or second-degree murder when they kill women they know, than women who kill men known to them. Women convicted of murder of a spouse or live-in mate frequently receive longer prison terms than men who kill wives or girlfriends, according to Browne.

The courts and juries perceive the killing of a domestic partner as an avoidable danger, and determine that the self defense act was "premeditated." Juries have not always had the education or the sensitivity to recognize that the female victim's instinct indicated that *this* time the batterer intended to complete his murderous act. If ever expert witnesses are needed, it is in defense of battered women who kill to save their own or their children's lives.

Always tell the truth

If you are charged after an act of self defense, your job and the job of your defense team is to give the jury the *truth*—the information and the account that shows you acted in response to threat of death or crippling injury. The responsibility for the death must be convincingly placed on the shoulders of the perpetrator. Elements of the defense should include specific information about your training—both marksmanship training and studies in judicious use of lethal force.

Prove that you faced a lethal threat. Demonstrate that you were forced to choose: your life or his continued violence. From your first report to the responding officer through the testimony you give in the courtroom, you must always tell the truth. Lies and exaggerations will be uncovered, and when one untruth is revealed, every statement you make becomes dubious. Your justified act of self defense will be tarnished and forever suspect.

---

[1] Browne, Angela, *When Battered Women Kill*, The Free Press, Division of Macmillan, Inc., 1987 pp. 11, 12.

4

Post-Violent Event Trauma:

After you live to tell about it

A *victim* who shoots in self defense must survive in several arenas—legal, emotional and physical. The media dissects self defense shootings with little regard for the victim's feelings; the courts argue the circumstances and question the victim's actions; and the victim herself must come to terms with the assault and her act of killing. You don't hear much about the emotional recovery from a violent event. I intentionally emphasized the word "victim" in the first sentence. It is difficult to equate "victim" with "survivor," yet the person who is forced to pull the trigger in self defense is victim, survivor, and victor, all at the same time.

The emotional aftermath is largely a product of our society's reaction to taking life, exacerbated by the body's response to the monumental stress of a life-death confrontation. The seminal work on post-violent event trauma is that of Dr. Walter Gorski. Though he has published no books, his studies have been distilled and taught by leading instructors like Massad Ayoob and John Farnam, and are the basis for this chapter. A "must-see" reference is Calibre Press' video *Ultimate Survivors* which reenacts the stories of four law enforcement professionals who survived deadly assaults and lived to relate their experiences and to discuss the aftermath.

The aftermath

After a self defense shooting, the survivor's body must withdraw from a major dose of adrenaline—the fight-or-flight chemical the body produces to power through an emergency. Ayoob comments that people chat about adrenaline as if it was a double espresso, just a boost in energy. Adrenaline, or epinephrine, he points out in lecture, is the substance doctors inject into the heart muscle to get it started when patients die. This powerful substance takes hours to leave the body, and the side effects are the some of the first post-violent event trauma symptoms the survivor experiences. Directly after the shooting, adrenaline in the body leaves the defender agitated, in a heightened mental state that may be followed by nausea or lethargy.

Traumatic events put a different perspective on day-to-day needs like food and sleep. Sleeplessness is common, and may continue for several nights. Having just survived a brush with death, the mind is unwilling to fall into a state of vulnerable unconsciousness. Likewise, loss or exaggeration of appetite is a common occurrence after a lethal encounter. The mind, trying to grasp the idea that it nearly perished, rejects the body's needs as if to say, "Who could eat at a time like this?"

Nightmares are common to those surviving a violent event, as the mind deals with the brush with death or the horror of killing. The dreams are often terrifying replays of the shooting, with endless variations, bizarre twists and conclusions. The attacker may become a loved one at the moment the bullets are loosed; the gun may become a different object in your hand; or the bullets may have no effect. Daydreams or flashbacks also replay the event. Survivors generally suffer insomnia, first as the adrenaline leaves the body, and later as the mind sorts through the fear and the memory of the attack.

Alcohol or drug dependency is a pitfall, as the survivor grasps "crutches" to help him or her through the hard times. A period of sexual dysfunction or promiscuity is experienced by many shooting survivors. Relationships and marriages may fall apart after a shooting. In addition to sexual difficulties, the relationship maybe challenged by the survivor's need for introspection, which excludes the partner who wants to assist in the loved one's recovery. The survivor often feels emotionally isolated, that no one understands their questions and emotions.

The isolation increases if friends stop visiting the survivor. They may not know how to interact with someone who has killed in self defense, or are afraid they will say something to upset the survivor. Those who act as if nothing has happened risk the survivor's outrage at the suggestion of fun or recreation. Some survivors become excessively careful and are afraid to leave their homes after a violent assault.

Casual acquaintances, business associates, and the general public are more obvious in their avoidance of one who has killed. Called the

"Mark of Cain" syndrome, this societal judgment on the survivor is evident in refusals to let the children play together, in cold shoulders at social functions, or in insensitive inquisitiveness as they try to understand "what kind of a person could kill someone." Unfortunately, we form our self-image largely from the reactions of other people. Repeatedly tell a child she is stupid and ugly, and she will grow up convinced she is stupid and ugly. Call a victim/survivor a murderer, and he or she will wonder if they are a cold-blooded killer.

Surviving a self defense shooting is a long and arduous process. Healing can be facilitated by skilled counseling, so if you face post violent event trauma, don't try to survive alone. A counselor, spiritual advisor or physician can give survivors solace and assistance during the emotional and physical recovery. *Do* seek help when the dreams, flashbacks and sleeplessness are ruining daily life; *do not* remain with a judgmental counselor or minister. There are good counselors available who have experience helping defense shooting survivors. Ask for professionals' names from the firearms instructors who trained you, or ask the mental health association for referral to a counselor with experience in post-violent event trauma. One of the best sources of relief is peer counseling, time spent with one who has also survived a killing and has dealt with the effects. Here is one who the survivor can trust to understand.

Most cities have rape crisis hotlines and support groups for women survivors. When you are ready, contact one of these groups and volunteer to help. The YWCA is a good starting place. If they don't have a program in place, the staff may be able refer you to a women's crisis group that will welcome your help.

Survivors who are treated by several professionals simultaneously occasionally receive conflicting medications, resulting in "pharmacological cascade." If receiving help from psychiatrists and physicians, tell each professional about other treatment, and advise them of prescriptions you have been given.

Survivors of self defense shootings are usually forever changed. Massad Ayoob compares the changes to scar tissue. For those able to grow from their experience, the trauma leaves behind a stronger character. Policeman Steve Chaney, featured in a segment of Calibre Press' *Ultimate Survivors*, relates his feelings after surviving a second line-of-duty shooting. At first he wondered, "why me?" But then he realized he was still alive, uninjured and thankful that he had not lost a partner. "Some of life's positive lessons are not learned in positive ways," he tells viewers.[1]

[1] *Ultimate Survivors*, Calibre Press, Inc., 666 Dundee Road, Suite 1607, Northbrook, ILL 60062-2727.

5

Safety-Conscious Attitudes

Animals *always* put their physical survival before legal or financial considerations. Much more in touch with instinctive survival tactics than are we, they often behave far more wisely in avoiding danger. Humans often deny the presence of danger, or if we acknowledge that threat exists, we follow that acknowledgment immediately by "I know, but...": "But I can't afford a reliable car." "But I can't afford an apartment in a safe, secure building." "But I can't pay for self defense training and a weapon."

Others who acknowledge the risk stop short of developing the level of skill required to deal with a lethal assault. Before I had lost too many karaté sparring matches to harbor this delusion any longer, I believed I could survive a one-on-one assault although I knew two or more could overpower me. I had to be thrown to the mat a number of times before acknowledging that *at that skill level*, I could easily be defeated.

After a woman acknowledges the danger, she needs to obtain the skills and weapons that will allow her to go where she needs, while behaving as safely as possible. What choices will she make that give her the maximum safety with the least restrictions? A hermit-like withdrawal from the vicissitudes of modern living is not practical. I am advising a very realistic assessment of the world we live in, and realistic decisions based on those dangers.

Ask yourself: what compromises am I willing to make to assure my well-being? Living outside the United States for a time, I developed the skill of blending in to avoid the hassles faced by a woman traveling alone. That habit, plus growing older and caring less what others think, has made it easier for me to adopt a comfortable style of dress that doesn't scream out for attention. Understand this: if attention is what you want, be assured you will receive it from one and all, not just from sane, desirable people. I'm not advocating homeliness, but I am talking about reserving your Spandex® for the gymnasium, your halter top for home, and pulling on a t-shirt and other inconspicuous garments for street wear.

Predatory people have an instinctive ability to sniff out those they can overpower. They observe body posture and levels of alertness. Female victims have several types of posture. A weak, submissive personality that will never put up a fight is typified by rounded shoulders, a lowered head and poor eye contact. Another is the flamboyant beauty, who puts lots of emphasis on outward appearance, but is not alert to dangers around her. Her posture, gait and garments are intended to advertise sexual attractiveness. Both attract predator attention; while the first is frightened, the second is not sufficiently concerned.

Though few advance far enough in karaté to mount an effective self defense, the martial arts *can* change bodies and attitudes. Karaté was the catalyst that took me out of my timid, submissive body into an erect, aggressive posture. Though I do not believe that most fighting techniques could save my life in a lethal assault, I know my strong, confident posture has discouraged assailants. Martial arts awoke my awareness to danger and heightened sensory perceptions of my surroundings.

The characteristic that all vulnerable women share is an oblivion to threat. An oblivious woman will wander right into the arms of trouble, engrossed in conversation or simply lost in her own thoughts. Evolution may be to blame: men have been the aggressive hunters since the advent of the opposable thumb. Women were the gatherers—looking down and collecting the fruits of the earth. A hunter has to possess a predatory instinct about the resources and threats around him. This sense has not deserted men.

Nearly all the women I know suffer from a lack of awareness of the moment-to-moment situation around them. If you can't answer a pop-quiz about the area you passed through five minutes ago, you are caught in this oblivion. Inner contemplation is good, but not on the street where being lost deep in thought can mean losing your life. Thoughtlessness is not the same as inner peace. The woman who indulges in air-headed thoughtlessness experiences an immobilizing terror when danger surprises her. The stress of bare fear is debilitating, but the alertness of moment-to-moment awareness is invigorating and requires no additional energy to maintain. And be truthful—most adults who look "lost in the clouds" and absent-minded usually aren't contemplating nirvana, they are more often worried about a relationship, concerned about a bank balance or calculating how many more miles they can get out of the radials before they have to buy new tires! Now *that* is exhausting!

Absolute awareness

I call it absolute awareness: the acknowledgment that danger exists; the moment-to-moment watchfulness for threat; the commitment to protect myself from danger; and the skill and training to back up that commitment.

Many self defense instructors employ Colonel Jeff Cooper's color code to describe the states of awareness appropriate to different levels of threat. Col. Cooper, known to handgunners as the father of modern pistolcraft, adapted the color code from military operations during World War II, when radio-transmitted reports on troop conditions were subject to interception by the enemy. The code has been altered for civilians, and I like the version taught at Lethal Force Institute.

The author was privileged to meet Colonel Jeff Cooper at the 1994 SHOT Show in Dallas, Texas.

Condition White describes circumstances in which you are *completely oblivious to any threat*. One enters Condition White upon sleeping, or when indulging in the oblivion discussed earlier.

An attitude of *awareness to the potential for threat* even in the absence of any specific danger is **Condition Yellow**. Psychologists tell us that humans can spend all their waking hours in Condition Yellow with absolutely no detrimental effects. Indeed, Condition Yellow should be your mental state while driving, chopping up vegetables, or hammering a nail into the wall. You are not subject to any active threat, but you are aware that your activity includes the potential for danger.

Some situations are riskier than others. Circumstances may cause you to switch into **Condition Orange.** This attitude is appropriate in

In Condition Orange, we acknowledge an increased degree of risk. Returning home to an empty house, this woman checks for dangers both outside and within the home before setting aside her holster purse.

situations that entail a *higher degree of risk* like driving on icy roads or walking down a dark alley at night in a risky part of town. In this mental state, all your senses are active, scanning for potential danger. You are prepared to take the appropriate action should a specific threat appear.

If three armed hoodlums approach you in the dark alley, you should switch to **Condition Red**, in which you have *identified a specific source of life-threatening danger*.

If Condition Red is embodied in the thought "Oh, no, they *could* hurt me!" Then **Condition Black** is "Oh, my goodness, they are assaulting me!" Black indicates a *lethal assault in progress* and justifies immediate use of deadly force to stop the assault.

How does your gun fit into these conditions? In Condition White you should not have a gun with you, since your lack of alertness makes the weapon available to a hostile. In Condition Yellow you may or may not have your gun available, but if you do have a gun, you must not drift into Condition White. In Condition Orange it would be preferable to have immediate access to your gun, or alternative defenses, like a slathering Rottweiler at your side. The gun may or may not be in your hand, depending on the situation. In Condition Red the gun should be in your hand if circumstances permit. You need to be ready and able to use it if a lethal assault pushes you into Condition Black.

Guns won't keep you safe

What? A book about guns saying that a gun won't keep you safe? Yep. Absolute awareness about your surroundings, tactical planning, and ability with an appropriate weapon are the factors that will keep you alive and well. *You* are the active party—your gun is an inert piece of machinery, incapable of any action on its own.

A $1,000 gun tricked out with all the modifications and improvements is useless if the owner is oblivious to the incoming threat, and indeed that fine weapon may be taken away and used against the unprepared owner. The prepared person, however, in addition to maintaining an appropriate level of awareness, will study and practice self defense tactics. In following chapters, we'll talk about basic tactical awareness and self defense.

Of husbands and significant others

Self defense trainers tell me that the women most reluctant to embrace a defensive art (be that a martial art or the handgun) are those who feel secure in their marriage or relationship. I suspect that relying on a mate for personal safety indicates a daughter-like dependency that characterizes other aspects of the relationship. Both the man and the woman contribute to the equilibrium of the relationship; the woman's move away from father-daughter dependency as she accepts responsibility for her own survival may threaten the union as it exists and require a new balance. Accepting responsibility challenges the woman's self-image as much as it challenges her perception of her strong male mate (to say nothing of *his* self-image as the strong male mate!) Ultimately, the woman who accepts responsibility for her own safety and survival may subsequently have to accept other life-skill responsibilities that she might simply prefer to leave to the man of the family.

The same trainers reporting the married-woman-hesitancy phenomenon also report that newly divorced women are often their most enthusiastic students. It makes perfect sense. The newly independent person learns to enjoy many new challenges; providing for her own survival offers a lot of strength, positive self-image and pride.

Thankfully, some women have genuinely good men who *encourage* them to exercise independence and develop survival skills. The woman fortunate enough to be involved with such a man has a responsibility to take care of herself and their family. It's not fair to place all the responsibility for mutual survival on one person—especially when the defender will be away at work one- to two-thirds of each day. This is not a responsibility—this is a con job. It says "You have to take care of me, even if I don't take care of myself." And that, I say, is bullshit.

6
Victory is a Fight Avoided

Women are rarely prepared to respond instantly to assault—it is a huge shock to find a punch coming toward your face. Mental preparedness (coupled with physical training) avoids or wins the battle. As discussed in foregoing chapters, the street is no place to lapse into Condition White.

Know who and what is around you. Practice this exercise: when driving or walking, train yourself to see all the details, all the people, doorways, windows. Mentally re-create the scene you just passed through as though preparing a movie stage. In your mind, describe the people within 15 to 20 feet; describe cars and structures; detail objects you could use as bullet-stopping cover in a gunfight. As awareness of the scene ahead and around you becomes habitual, you'll rarely be frightened by the wino who lurches out of the doorway to ask for money. You will already have moved to the outside of the sidewalk, or possibly insulated yourself among other pedestrians.

Walk purposefully, head up, eyes scanning your surroundings. Keep your hands free so you are ready to fight if surprised. Don't shove your hands into pockets or wrap your arms around your torso. Don't carry a big purse or occupy your arms with packages. Keep your limbs supple and relaxed. A tense "gunfighter's claw" responds slowly, but relaxed limbs can respond lightning quick. Stay loose and alert.

Make eye contact with other pedestrians. Let potential assailants know you have *recognized* them. Abusers prefer anonymity. Walk away from catcalls, unwanted comments or questions.

One of the harsh facts of life in the '90s has been the massive proliferation of people living on the city streets. The presence of these poor, desperate people has drastically altered the mood of the streets in most American cities. I was out of the United States from January through July of 1990. When I returned to the States that summer, I took up residence near downtown Seattle. Imagine my surprise to encounter nearly as many beggars in my first morning stroll as I would have on a walk to the vegetable market in India! But there was a difference: the Seattle beggars were physically aggressive. They took offense if ignored, some would physically block the sidewalk or verbally insult those ignoring their demands. Some worked in pairs, flanking the person they had targeted. It would be wrong to blame all the street crime on homeless people; many of the predators "working" streets and city parks do not share the street dweller's fate.

Learn a few basic rules for dealing with aggressive approaches from strangers:

Whether in Asia or America, one of the most common approaches a criminal makes is asking an innocent question. A stranger will approach you in a parking lot as you unlock your car. "Excuse me, do you have a match?" Open the car door before the stranger gets too close, quickly enter the safety of a locked car, and only then, only if you feel strongly compelled, should you respond. The problem is, it never ends with the first question. The predator prolongs the exchange, asking other questions about landmarks, anything to distract you until they have a chance to slip through your defenses and get what they want— your possessions or your person.

Create distance between you and the stranger and respond firmly "Sorry, I don't smoke," as you leave the area. Experience tells me that ignoring a harasser is usually perceived as fearfulness. Answer forcefully that you cannot help them, while you quickly get into a safer position. Assaults happen lightening fast--usually in three to five seconds. Too often the female victim is knocked to the ground before she realizes what is happening.

Where is it written that you have to be nice to strangers? The Bible was written for another time, not 1990s street encounters that endanger your life. I firmly believe that the Creator placed an excellent survival instinct in all His creatures, and would prefer you and I exercise that instinct to assure our daily survival. Today's reality requires a guarded response to strangers. Giving help to those in need is admirable, but it must be accomplished in sensible, safe ways.

One of our century's mass killers, Alton Coleman, helped by accomplice Debra Denise Brown, reached a number of victims by asking for rides to church or prayer meetings. The victims were robbed, raped and usually murdered by the opportunistic pair. The well-known serial rapist-murderer Theodore Bundy accomplished his first double-murder by asking women at Lake Sammammish, near Seattle, to help him load a boat onto his car. He wore an arm sling, and after capturing one young woman with this ruse, returned and successfully abducted a second victim. It is thought the young women watched him rape one another, and one likely witnessed the murder of the other, before being killed herself.

First, recognize the predatory stalking technique of stepping in close to engage the victim in conversation. There are phone numbers to call for the correct time; directions can be obtained by reading maps or asking

The predatory approach is sometimes marked by a stranger's simple request for a match.

at gas stations. Two muggings at an apartment building where I lived occurred when a man approached and asked for directions while our residents were unlocking the front door. One woman lost her purse for her courtesy; the other found herself wrestling with a man who threw her to the ground as she gave directions to a public park.

If circumstances don't allow an immediate escape from your stalker, face your harasser and order "Go away! Don't talk to me!" or "Leave me alone, *now*." Couple your command with forceful eye contact. Your unwavering eye contact shows your assailant you are not afraid to take whatever action is necessary to rid yourself of him. Use a firm, commanding voice, in a low, controlled tone, expelling the words with air from the diaphragm. The first women's self defense course I took many years ago, taught us to cuss and swear at assailants. Role-playing a stalking event, the victim was to swing around and yell "What do you want, asshole? Leave me the fuck alone." The premise was that the bad language would shock the harasser into breaking off the pursuit. Experience has since shown that gutter language angers the assailant and escalates the assault. Your abusive language will also be perceived by witnesses as active involvement in a two-sided dispute.

A young advertising professional with whom I worked learned this lesson the hard way. What began as a purse-snatching attempt rapidly escalated to an all-out assault when she screamed obscenities at a man who initially only wanted her wallet. She had been knocked to the ground and would have sustained a beating, but a Seattle police officer rounded the corner and stopped the assault before she was badly hurt. Your pre-emptive strength lies in unwavering eye contact, aggressive attitude and body language, not in bravado expressed by foul language. In all instances, you must be able to back up your *attitude* with your skill and your weapon.

If your assailant disobeys your command to leave, take evasive action. In crowded public spaces, uninvolved bystanders can serve as a distraction while you get away. Step around other pedestrians so they and others *have* to step between you and your harasser, giving you time to escape. Other urban features that provide escape routes are malls, stores and public buildings. Here, you can find a telephone and call for police help.

Even if you carry the firepower to "win" a fight, you must avoid engaging an opponent in battle unless the threat to your life is immediate and unavoidable. One winter evening I waited with a companion at a Seattle bus stop. Several others gathered to wait for the bus, including a small-statured fellow who began "working" the crowd. In parts of Seattle, begging is a normal activity and people tend to forget the danger it can pose. We rebuffed the fellow, only to become re-involved when he began to touch a young woman who couldn't seem to fend him off.

In retrospect, intervention may have been foolhardy, but we stepped in and moved the man into the street. As his verbal abuse escalated, he reached under his coat for the weapon he kept in the small of his back. At that moment, the bus arrived. Keeping one eye on him, we took seats toward the front of the bus. To my horror, he boarded, took a seat at the very front of the bus and started threatening to "cut up some rich young yuppies." When the bus driver refused to discharge the man, I decided to disembark at the next busy, well-lit stop. I told my companion that I intended to get past the threatening man *using others for cover*. When a trio of college-age boys came forward to leave, I also arose and made a safe exit, keeping the uninvolved boys between me and the harasser.

Had I owned a gun, I would have made the same decision. There are *no* winners in a street fight. At close quarters a gun against a knife will not save you. The knifer may die from your bullet, but not before he has cut you with his blade.

Jim Cirillo, of NYPD Stake Out Squad fame, told me that he didn't consider the gun a superior weapon in a close-range gun-knife battle. "The knife doesn't run out of bullets," he pointed out. The knifer can cut you terribly before your bullets shut him down, Cirillo stressed.

Street fights are further complicated by the presence of innocent bystanders. My bullet might have passed through the vagrant to kill the bus driver or others. And finally, having finessed our way out of the situation, we were free to go. Had we fought, we could have been held accountable for his injuries. Always try to escape a confrontation; join the fight only if the alternative is death or crippling injury.

React decisively if your instincts tell you something's wrong. If you feel scared or uneasy, leave the area. Be prepared to react immediately if you are assaulted. A small .38 revolver in your pocket, a can of oleoresin capsicum or a mini-baton and keys in your hand, may deflect an assailant long enough for you to reach safety.

Choose your pleasures

A woman needs to weigh the events she attends to determine if it entails a greater-than-ordinary threat because of location or the type of crowd. Is the level of threat manageable under the circumstances of the

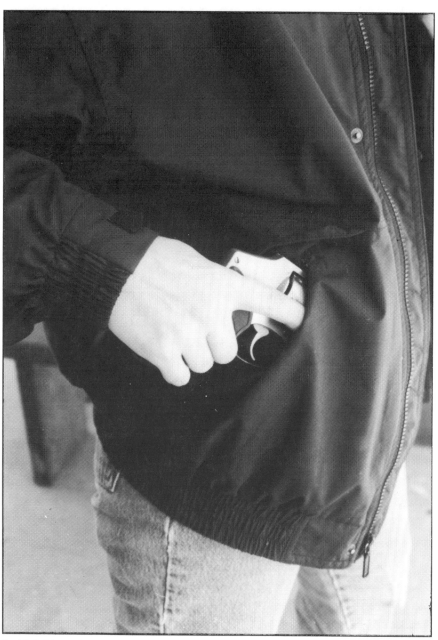

Smith & Wesson's Centennial revolver can be carried alone in a pocket for very fast access.

event? For example, I might skip a rock concert, since concert security personnel usually frisk spectators, making it impossible to carry a weapon. I might choose not to attend a theater production held in a neighborhood with a high crime rate. These decisions are extensions of awareness and acknowledgments that threats exist. They represent the mindset embodied in Condition Yellow, where you are ready to avoid things that might cause you harm. Choose your dangers. For example, I despise those huge multi-floor concrete parking garages. I'm not the only one who feels at risk going there. A clerk at a gun range told me that after feeling threatened in a hospital's underground parking facility he started parking on the street or in an open-air lot.

If you must park in public garages, walk out in the driving lane, avoiding the close confines between parked cars, and have your gun *immediately* accessible. Park in a garage with live attendants and drive right back out if *anything* feels threatening once you are inside. Park near the attendant, in a brightly lit area. If you are delayed at work, ask a trusted co-worker or a security officer you know and trust to escort you to your car. Follow your instincts, they will keep you alive. Parking garages don't generate enough foot traffic for the relative safety of crowds, and aren't patrolled nearly well enough to deter the opportunistic criminal looking for a victim.

Public elevators are another spot where I exercise a guarded care. A few years ago, I'm told, numerous Seattle women began using the stairs after a series of muggings and molestations in the downtown high-rise elevators. These ladies exercised (no pun intended) admirable awareness of danger, and probably got a little extra muscle tone as a bonus. Seriously, give me a crowded elevator, with all its discomforts, instead of an elevator car containing only one or two people. It is another situation-specific decision, but there have been several incidents like the one at a Seattle community college when I boarded an elevator alone, only to be followed in by a fellow who I had seen waiting nearby. I can't say exactly what alarmed me about him, demeanor, eyes or actions. But I exercised the "be smart and act like an idiot" option, pressing the door open button and saying, "Silly me! I don't need to go up!"

Don't board an elevator with a single occupant; wait for the next car. When you get in an elevator, stand near the control panel so you can activate the alarm for help. In elevators have a weapon in hand: a revolver in the pocket, your Persuader mini-baton on your keys.

I see women taking more risks while jogging and exercising than during any other activity. Women exercise along deserted running paths, in parks replete with excellent hiding spots, and wearing garments that might be construed by a courtroom lawyer as an invitation to rape. Again, I don't advocate locking yourself away in a cloister: I do suggest responsible awareness. If possible, walk or jog with several companions and a reliable guard dog. Even in groups, maintain awareness of your surroundings, don't drift off in a haze of aching muscles or raucous music from your sports radio. I would not cut off my auditory warning system by wearing headphones in public.

Jogging paths are a more difficult subject. Many of the running paths follow remote, scenic, yet dangerous routes. Bushes, trees and ravines offer cover for an assailant and a place where he may drag his victims. In urban areas jog on a public track around an open playing field. And use the track only during daylight and at times when other people are about. In Spokane, Washington, Kevin Coe enjoyed a lengthy career as a rapist, preying on solitary joggers who ran at night or in the quiet of early morning.

Let me re-emphasize the importance of immediate access to your handgun whenever you are out in public. Shop for a good concealment holster, or carry your gun in a holster-fanny pack or a gun purse tucked snugly against your body. A concealed-hammer revolver like Smith & Wesson's Centennial line, can be hidden in a pocket with your hand on it, ready for immediate use if your awareness rises to Condition Red.

Automobile safety AAA never told you about

The aware woman uses everyday items to maintain her safety. A locked car surrounds you with an added ring of safety if you are alert to tactical advantages. Maintaining a safe car that will not fail you is critical. This, as with home safety, is a matter of priorities. Forego buying a few CDs, in favor of getting a tune up. Keep the gas tank more than a quarter full, so you don't absent-mindedly run out of gas and get stranded. Learn basic car maintenance skills, like changing tires. The ability to replace a flat tire and get your car to a tire repair store greatly increases your safety. If you cannot repair the car's problem, do not leave the safety of your locked car. If you have a cellular phone, dial 911 to summon help. If not, turn on the emergency flashers and wait for the state patrol. Do not open the door or window for anyone but an identified law enforcement officer. If, for any reason, you are unsure of the officer's legitimacy, remain in the car. Direct the individual to call a tow truck.

Your safety begins before you get in the car. Your personal vehicle should always remain locked, even when you are in it. Before entering, check between the seats for an intruder. Once in the car, lock all the doors to keep unwanted "passengers" out. Never pick up hitch hikers.

When you are stopped at a traffic light, glance around to see who and what is within striking distance. At traffic lights, maintain distance between your car and the one ahead. A good visual cue is to stay far enough back to see the rear tires of the car ahead. This space will allow you to pull around the car ahead and get away from an assailant. Tony Scotti's video tape on "defensive" driving is an excellent source of information. While Scotti addresses the driver/bodyguard's responsibilities, protecting yourself and your family is equally important and the material taught is applicable.[1]

While driving remain alert to cars that may be following you. Taking

Taken from inside the car, this photo the shows the safe distance behind another vehicle at a traffic light to allow a rapid escape if attacked in your car.

down a license plate number, and checking in the rear view mirror, will often frighten an opportunistic assailant. If you are followed, *do not* go home. Go to the nearest public facility, park as close to the door as possible and run inside, calling out loudly, "Call the police, I'm being followed!"

If you are assailed while stopped in traffic, take any escape route available—at times like this its OK to break traffic laws. Obviously, you will need to be aware of others, but a surprising number of people will sit at a red light and allow their window to be broken in by an assailant, before driving through an empty intersection or onto the sidewalk.

We have also been trained to get out of our cars if involved in a fender bender. Predators recognize this training as an opportunity. The rapist causes a minor accident and when you leave the safety of your car to inspect the damage, he takes you. You must remain in your car and either wait for the police to arrive, or drive to a busy, well-lit area and report the incident from a safe place. I am not at all certain I would get out of my car if a second motorist stopped to assist. I would ask the "Good Samaritan" to go call for help, and would remain locked inside my car until the police arrived. Under no conditions should you get out of your car if only you and the other driver are on the scene. If you have

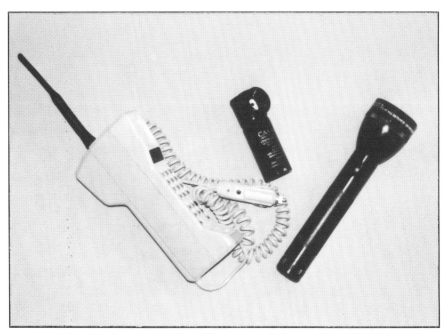

Carry a cellular phone in your car with which to summon help, as well as a flashlight and pepper spray in case you must leave your car before it is repaired.

to leave the safety of your car, get out with a can of pepper spray in your hand or your hand on a revolver in your pocket.

Never stop to help what appears to be a stranded motorist. You simply cannot know their disposition or true identity. If you feel you should help, call the police who will respond and help those who are truly stranded. One of the best safety tools you can have in your car is a portable cellular phone. If you become lost or your car stalls, the cellular phone lets you summon help without leaving the safety of your vehicle. It is an excellent way to call for help if you are involved in a minor accident. It is also useful if you see a family stranded and want to summon assistance without endangering yourself.

This same concept holds true for walking situations. Never go close to someone who calls out for help—assess the situation cautiously from a safe distance and call out that you have heard their cries and are going now to summon the police. The call for help is frequently a ploy of rapists, who may cry out that they have just been assaulted and injured. The rapist grabs the woman who comes to his aid.

If you use a metro bus system, try to maintain a schedule that lets you stay off the bus after dark. If that's not possible, wait for the bus and get

An aerosol can of oleoresin capsicum (pepper spray) is easily stored on the visor of the automobile, and is in easy reach of the driver for emergency use.

off at stops that are busy and well-lit. On the bus, be alert, know who is on the bus, what they're doing and how close they are to you. Try to sit in the front near the driver. When leaving the bus, watch to see who exits with you. If evasive action like crossing a street several times does not separate your follower, run to the nearest well-lit area and rush into a busy restaurant or grocery store, yelling, "Help! Call the police! I'm being followed. Call the police!"

In every situation, the aware woman will ask herself, "Does it feel safe?" She will mentally explore the potential for danger before committing herself to any action. For example, if asked to visit the apartment of a new male friend, the aware woman will probably respond that she is sorry, she cannot, but may offer an invitation to get together in a restaurant or other public location. A responsible man will recognize her prudence without taking offense; a predator will act insulted and exhibit hurt feelings or will ridicule her caution. Consider this is a good chance to find out whether or not your new friend will respect your intelligence and sensibility.

We have to take responsibility for creating our own safe zones. We must not blithely wander into another's control. A full, secure life is possible; we need only take responsibility for our own well being.

---

[1] Scotti, Tony, *Counterambush Driving Skills and Evasion Techniques,* © Paladin Press, P.O. Box 1307, Boulder, CO 80306 (303) 443-7250.

7
Don't Compromise on Safety

Make personal safety your number one priority. This requires an investment in safe living quarters, assuring the road worthiness of your car, and budgeting for self defense equipment and training. The year I began shooting, my wardrobe came from Goodwill, because my training and ammunition budget took precedence over new suits and dresses.

One woman with whom I went through several classes would argue with instructors about safe housing arrangements, saying she was unable to take any of the suggested safety precautions in her low-priced apartment. She drove a beautiful classic Mercedes, affordable because she skimped on rent. I, too, went through a time when my living quarters were completely unsafe—a cheap basement apartment with un-barred windows. Looking back, I must admit that I was spending the additional $50 to $100 a month I needed for safer housing, to host a jobless friend. I thought I couldn't spend the additional money on safer housing, and I know a number of other women say the same thing. We need to hard-headedly assess our expenditures to find that $50 to $100 a month for safer quarters.

When you look for a new home or apartment, look at the security provisions and study the potential danger spots. Every apartment layout differs. Use your survival awareness to check out potential threats. The presence or absence of security measures like dead-bolt locks and window bars gives you a measure of the landlord's commitment to tenant well-being. The superintendent of an apartment building with good security measures should check out the references and background of those to whom he or she rents, reducing your threat from unsavory neighbors. Find a secure building, where only residents have access through the locked doors, and raise Cain if someone is violating that security measure by blocking doors open for visitors or their own convenience. When you rent, demand bars on ground-level windows or lease an apartment without ground-level access to windows or doors. Most municipal codes require landlords to provide dead-bolt locks on doors, not just locking doorknobs. If the landlord snorts when you ask why these security devices are absent, look for another place to rent!

Home security

Every now and then, a newspaper carries a story about someone who rose in their sleep and fired a bullet...into themselves. These poor souls are the victims of their own lack of training, or of bad advice from an untrained sort who said, "If you can't get to your gun instantly, it won't be any help if someone breaks into your house at night!" You'll hear no snickering from me as I relate this truth: I was a sucker for that advice, and until better trained, I slept with a loaded, unholstered gun on my bed headboard. I was then living in a basement studio apartment with ground-level windows without bars, and I believed the threat great enough to justify the potential for disaster at my own hands.

This is the first premise of home defense: If your home can be breached so easily and rapidly that you must be able to make an instantaneous response to danger, the problem is not how to assure that you can respond quickly, the problem is how to strengthen the perimeter of safety around your home! If you feel you are unable to provide safe housing, re-assess your personal priorities and analyze your own lack of commitment to your safety and well-being.

Even in upscale housing, a sensible person can take precautions to increase the safety perimeter around their home. A good-quality security alarm is the first choice, but a number of secondary and companion safety provisions are also recommended. Entrances should have solid-core doors fitted with dead-bolt locks with bolts that reach far into the door frame. Long strike plate screws need to tap into the door frame studs. Exterior doors generally open inward. If they open outward, be sure the hinges are not installed on the outside, where anyone can pop out the pins and pull the door off its hinges. A wide-angle peep hole lets you assess the identity and number of people outside. Windows need sturdy metal or heavy wood frames, also fitted with locks.

Sliding windows, especially those in older wood frames, can be made more secure by adding a removable 1"x2" stick the height of the movable window pane. After several break-ins at an old apartment building where I once lived, the police told us that the burglars were inserting a wedge of wood or metal at the base of the window frame, then depressing the wedge to create enough leverage to break out the lock at the top of the window frame. There was no noise of shattering glass, only the pop as the lock broke free from the old wooden window frame.

A number of lesser deterrents make an empty home or apartment less inviting to intruders. A TV or radio playing gives the initial impression of occupancy, as do one or two lights left on in the home. If away for an extended time, use electric timers to cycle lights in different parts of the home. I would not depend solely on either practice, but neither would I ignore their contribution to overall security. As part of its "CrimeStrike" campaign, the National Rifle Association has a small stock of intermediate motion alarm and lighting products to shore up home security.[1]

After an Edmonds, Washington, woman survived a rape, then got to her gun and held the man for police, another local woman remarked to

A deadbolt lock must extend at least one to two inches into a solid door frame to deter a determined house breaker.

television reporters: "I'm so glad they caught him. It's getting warm and I need to be able to leave my sliding patio door open again." In hot weather, intruders often find houses open and waiting for them. While you are awake and alert, open doors and windows require a higher level of awareness, but when you lapse into Condition White—asleep, in the shower or other activities that take your awareness off the perimeters—you need to lock doors and windows accessible from the ground. Close up and secure your home before leaving—whether going on a quick errand to the store or leaving for a day at work. An empty house with open windows is quite an invitation to those who would take your possessions or pounce on you when you return.

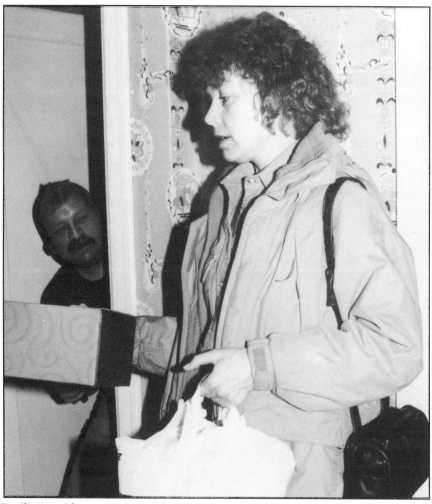

Familiarity with your own home is little protection against a motivated attacker who is hidden, waiting to ambush you.

An absolute *must* for home safety is bright, well-placed lighting. Home security lighting systems range from gimmicky to great. Consult the experts. At a minimum be sure your doorways, garage and halls are well lit. If you park in a garage, either leave a light on when you depart, or install lighting you can turn on by remote control before you enter the garage. While living near downtown Seattle, I once avoided a prowler revealed by the light above the door. It was late when I guardedly approached the building door. As I drew within 20 feet, I saw a figure slip from the shadows, through the light's beam and back into the shadows between the building and an adjacent garage. Had I not seen the movement, I would have been within easy striking distance while unlocking the door. I don't know if that prowler meant any harm—I didn't stay around long enough to find out—but his furtive actions indicated his presence was not authorized. I sprinted away and used another entrance to the building, shaken by how easily I might have walked into range of danger.

When I enter my home at night, I pause after opening the front door to gather sensory impressions to see if anything is awry. If you have pets who customarily meet you at the door, their absence or demeanor can be an indicator. Stop and listen as you light the house, be aware of, and cautiously inspect places where intruders might be concealed.

A guard or watch dog can be a valuable addition to the security team, primarily as an early warning device. Don't put too much trust in a dog's ability to overpower intruders: one quiet .22 bullet in the head removes a canine obstacle. However, if your pooch faithfully greets you when you return home, its absence might be the first warning of danger.

Finally, let me emphasize the importance of not entering a house you believe has been breached by an intruder. House clearing is one of the most dangerous acts imaginable. Despite the fact that it is your "home turf," intruders have the upper hand because they have the element of surprise and can choose a tactically superior place to wait for you. You don't know where they are, if they are armed, or how many have intruded. Even if you immobilize one intruder, will you survive attacks by others backing up the one you stopped?

If you find your home has been broken into, don't enter the house. Go elsewhere and call the professionals, police or sheriff officers who can search with trained dogs and other appropriate equipment while you wait outside in tax-funded safety.

The bump in the night

There are many concerns if your home is broken into while you are present. Everyone has been wakened from sound sleep by a shattering or bumping noise. You sit up and try to determine the source of the noise—is it merely your four-year-old trying to get a drink of water, a pet scratching at the door, or has a burglar entered?

This is one self defense instance where immediate action is inadvisable. You need the ensuing moments to listen further to determine the source of the noise. Your four-year-old will most likely call out or act in their usual way, letting you know that rushing out to confront this particular noise, gun in hand, is a very, very poor idea. Even if your house has been entered, there are many reasons not to seek out the intruder and shoot. Could an innocent person be in your home without your knowledge? Do your teenagers have friends they might allow to come in and sleep off too much beer? Do any friends, relatives or other innocent people have keys to your home? Your best friend may have had a midnight fight with her boyfriend and decided to spend the night on your couch without waking you up. Have you given her a chance to identify herself before she meets you and your gun in the hallway? I once came within seconds of pointing a .38 revolver at a building manager who let herself into my apartment without knocking, assuming that I was away.

If I knew the noises were not caused by family members or guests, and continued movement and noise convinced me that an intruder was inside, I would set up my tactical HQ in the bedroom and dial the emergency number. Evan Marshall suggests putting 911 or your police emergency number on speed dial. When you call, give the police dispatcher the following message:

"There is an intruder in my home at 100 Center Street. I believe he is on the first floor; I will wait on the second floor. I am a white female, 5'5" and have on a red bathrobe. I am armed with a snub-nosed revolver. I repeat, there is an intruder in my home..."

The unreliability of telecommunications dictates that you state your address first, describe the situation, then give additional details. Make the message brief and to the point, then repeat the information. Experts advise you to stay on the line with the emergency dispatcher so you can verify the responding officers' identity by asking the dispatcher if the unit has arrived at your address. Locked in your bedroom, it is wise to refuse entry to anyone you cannot positively identify as a law enforcement officer. If it becomes necessary to protect yourself or family members from the intruder, you may have to break off communications with the dispatcher or leave the safe room. Every self defense situation is unique in itself, and you will have to remain fluid and able to make decisions based on the circumstances.

Why offer your personal description and reveal that you are armed? Two reasons. Law enforcement agencies will respond rapidly to a scene where they know at least one firearm is involved—the presence of a deadly weapon tells them this is an explosive situation. The personal description is vital. You may be mistaken for a house breaker in the surprise and confusion as the police arrive and search out the first person who looks threatening.

After calling for help, you have two choices. You can remain silently ensconced in your safe room, taking cover behind a bullet-stopping obstacle, weapon in hand. You may choose to call out to the intruder: "Intruders: The police have been called and are on their way. We are armed. Leave the house immediately and we will not harm you!" In either event, do not leave the safety of your room unless the safety of children or others is threatened.

Evan Marshall suggests a more direct approach. His version of the challenge is, "Get out!" delivered in command voice. He strongly recommends setting up the home so the defender can wait, firearm in hand, at the head of a stairwell or a hall, shutting off access to the rest of the family.

The problems with seeking out and confronting a housebreaker are legion. Even though you know your own home layout, the intruder has the advantage of surprise. You simply cannot know where he has hidden. You have become the prey, as you search your own home, and your responses will be in *reaction* to the intruder's actions. He is running the game and you will likely be at his mercy.

The only reason to leave your safe room is to ensure your children's safety. Call the police, then pad quietly from room to room, gathering up the smaller ones. Wake the older children with the instruction to remain exactly where they are and lock them safely in their rooms, unless you believe the intruder may gain access to that child's room before you or the police can intercept them. Other times, the emergency may make it necessary to secure the safety of family members before calling the authorities.

In a two-story home, if all the bedrooms are on the upper floor, take a place of strategic control at the head of the stairs. This denies a hostile any access to the vulnerable sleeping areas, and the intruder must come through your gunfire before he can reach those you love.

In establishing a "safe" room, replace the door with a solid-core door with a good dead-bolt lock. Include a cellular phone for outside communication if the intruder cuts your phone lines. The phone can be

A large, 6'3" man can hide in a child's toy closet. Don't overlook small places when studying the danger zones in your home.

the same one you carry in your car. When you come home, go straight to your safe room and place your wallet or purse, keys and portable phone in the same place each time.

Practice fields

How strange that we practice musical skills, our tennis game, and for Toastmasters club, but we do not practice scenarios to ingrain skills to ensure our own survival.

An example exercise would be taking a run through your house or apartment when all the other occupants are gone. Starting at your car or front door, enter, looking carefully for all the spots where an assailant might hide. You may decide to install better lighting, move or trim certain bushes, or clear boxes and debris in your garage that could conceal assailants. Entering your home, check for alcoves or closets where an assailant might hide. Check for fast access to light switches.

Moving through your home, be aware of lanes of movement—advantages for both you and a housebreaker. Be aware of heavy furniture that would provide you cover in a gunfight, and conversely, look for places where an assailant might hide. You might choose to relocate a large, packed bookshelf to a strategic position for bullet-stopping cover. You might choose to rearrange furniture to impede unauthorized entry through a window or sliding glass door. You should be sure the location of a waterbed or a large, packed chest of drawers provides bullet-stopping cover in your bedroom. Crouch or lay down behind the furniture to be sure it is large enough to conceal and protect your body.

Families with children should assign bedrooms so the armed adults protect the halls leading to the bedrooms, taking the room at the head of the hallway or assigning the children to upstairs bedrooms, if the sleeping rooms are on both first and second floors.

Another exercise that can be conducted with a bit more levity, is one suggested by Massad Ayoob in his excellent book, *In the Gravest Extreme.* He recommends playing a game of hide-and-seek with your children. They know all the best hiding places, and he says, any place your four-foot child can hide offers concealment to a motivated, full-size house breaker. Again, you might rearrange the furniture if you find a very risky point from which an intruder might spring on you.

For renters, apartment halls and doorways are excellent places to practice your survival awareness. How many times have you rounded a corner in a public hallway, in the grip of a daydream or a worry, and gasped as you almost collided with a neighbor? Learn not to walk blithely around blind corners or into laundry rooms or utility closets. Walk out and around 90° corners, open doors fully and look in before entering. Use these utilitarian moments as training grounds to sharpen your awareness—a skill that may some day protect you from an assailant.

Your safety depends on knowing who is in a public space such as an elevator or laundry room before you commit yourself to entering. Learn, by daily practice, to scan the room, including behind the door you just opened, to ascertain who else occupies the room. A door that opens against a wall can simply be pushed all the way open to check for anyone hiding behind it.

Paranoid or careful?

Does all the foregoing sound a little paranoid? Some mistake a cautious person for a cringing paranoiac. And there is a big difference between a cringing, fear-ridden person and one who acknowledges the possibility of danger and takes steps to intercept anyone who would harm them or their family.

Are you safe inside?

It's easy to feel safe and let down our guard once we're inside the front door. Remember to lock the door behind you, and if it's dark, draw the blinds.

Never tell anyone at the door or on the phone that you're alone. If a caller insists he must "talk to the man of the house," stage a fictional conversation in which the "man" refuses to come to the phone. Train family members, especially children, never to tell who is home and who is out, when they'll return and how long they've been gone. Rapists and burglars use the telephone to gather information.

If you receive obscene phone calls, some groups recommend blowing a loud whistle into the receiver. The most important advice is to hang up immediately. Do not converse with the caller at all. If they've given any indication that they know any part of your daily schedule, home location, work or commute route, call the police immediately. If the calls continue, call the telephone company and notify the police of the continuing problem.

Rapists and burglars often disguise themselves as repair or utility workers. Require company identification and verify the identity with the utility company, your landlord or whoever sent the individual before letting them in your home. Once inside, stay in the same room with them while they perform their work. Have your firearm or self defense weapon on your person. Leave the worker standing on the porch, door locked, while you get the weapon, if necessary. If at any time their actions make you uneasy, tell them to leave. If they refuse, you will have to leave quickly and call the police from an outside location.

Initials, instead of your full name on the mailbox, telephone directory or other listings help protect you from people who prey on women. Don't use Ms., Mrs., or Miss or any thing else that indicates gender. When asked for a phone number by a sales clerk accepting your check, give a false number, a ruse suggested by Paxton Quigley, author of *Armed and Female*.[2] Even if the clerk seems benign, a member of the store staff or another shopper may use that information to harass you. Do not reveal your home address, telephone numbers or social security numbers.

Business women who need to give clients contact information need to rent an off-site mail box and phone service. Never list residential telephones or addresses on business cards or other promotional literature that you hand out. Even if you are careful to whom you give your card, you cannot control where it goes after it is out of your hands.

[1] National Rifle Association Market Place, (800) 233-5459, Ext. 1073.

[2] Quigley, Paxton, *Armed and Female*, released in paperback in 1990 by St. Martin's Press.

8
Intermediate Defenses

"I was asleep. He was on me so fast I didn't have time to do anything. Besides, he had a knife," said the first.

"He had my arms pinned down. I couldn't have used a gun even if I had one. All I could see was the Bible on the headboard of my bed, so I concentrated on it to keep my sanity while he raped me," another said later.

I was promoting self defense and firearms classes at a women's show, with an aggressive sign that asked, "Could You Stop a Rapist?" Relating their stories, both women needed to convince me—and themselves—that nothing could have prevented the rape they endured. Both spoke quietly for a few minutes, but dismissed the possibility that any fighting skills would have allowed them to escape. It cast a pall over the day; I felt sad that neither had been able to detect the rapist entering the house or stop his assault. I was further troubled that neither would consider preparing against the possibility of a second such situation.

Since you've made it this far in the book, you know that I value crime prevention more highly than killing an assailant who has attempted or completed a rape or violent physical assault. Safe housing, safe street behavior, and awareness of danger when you're in your car are among the first survival lessons I want to emphasize. Next, we need to realize that the gun is just a safety rescue tool, it won't *save* us unless we are prepared to use it, or know how to escape an assailant's restraint to gain that two to five seconds to draw and fire the weapon. Finally, the gun is not appropriate to deflect a minor threat; its use is justified only in situations where innocent life is in immediate danger of death or crippling injury. How preferable it would be to deter an assailant *before* the incident became life threatening, before a rape or violent assault occurs.

The weapon you always carry

Empty hand escapes and defenses should be mandatory training for all girls as they grow up. A girl's or woman's size should be no deterrent if the teacher is innovative, and the martial art selected is applicable to self defense. For example, Aikido techniques work on principles of leverage, so do not depend on weight or size to work against a larger assailant.

Women need a few basic skills they can learn in one to two months, with simple, direct techniques that can be practiced with friends or husbands. Some students will find the practice relaxing and empowering, and will continue formal classes. Though that is admirable, it is

An Aikido wristlock removes an assailant who is attempting a front grab.

unfair to deny defensive tactics and skills to students who won't commit years to their training.

In hand-to-hand defense, the defender must disable the assailant's ability to breathe or see, or cause harm to their limbs and extremities. "Disrupt wind, vision, or limbs," advises Phil Messina, founder of Modern Warrior.[1] When you evaluate a defensive art or weapon, ask if it accomplishes these, or at least two of these objectives.

Defense training is often scenario-specific. Women are usually advised to kick the assailant in the groin or jab him in the eyes. Both plans are fine if the assailant does not block the groin kick or reflexively deflect the jab to his eyes. Protecting eyes or the groin are natural reflexes that often prevent an eye stab or groin strike from connecting. A kick to the groin may not disable an assailant, and if it does not connect with forceful accuracy, it will just enrage an already violent combatant.

In unarmed combat, I'm a strong proponent of kicking defenses to break or injure limbs and joints or disrupt balance. Unlike men, female body strength is centered in the lower body and legs. A smashing kick to the side of the assailant's knee can break or disable the limb sufficiently for you to escape an attack from side or front. Even a kick and downward scrape to the shin can surprise someone making a rear grab enough for you to break free and escape.

If you are knocked to the ground, orient your head *away* from the assailant by spinning around on your back and derriere. Use your legs to kick and trap the assailant's legs. A strong leg trap can put the assailant on the ground while you spring to your feet to escape or draw a gun. If under attack, don't take time to kneel then stand up. Rock your body weight back on your shoulders, then rock forward onto your butt with one leg bent under you, the other bent perpendicular to the ground. As your weight shifts to butt and legs, use one elbow to push off the ground and rise to your feet on the leg that was perpendicular to the ground.

Women can often deliver a disorienting palm-heel smash to an assailant's face if they are grabbed from the front. Bending the knees and dropping the hips, then springing up into the palm-heel smash really empowers the blow.

Though I have some favorite empty hand techniques, this isn't the place to go deeply into unarmed defenses. Find a martial arts instructor willing to work with you on ground-fighting techniques (the skills needed by the women discussed at the beginning of the chapter), recovery skills to get back on your feet rapidly, choke-hold escapes, and wrist locks. Empty hand techniques you can perform naturally and reflexively can "buy" the seconds necessary to escape or draw a firearm.

Intermediate weaponry

An intermediate (non-lethal) weapon is meant to deflect an assault before it turns lethal, or to effect a temporary escape, creating time to draw and use the firearm. The intermediate weapon is not an appropriate response to a lethal force attack. Using a gun is justified only when murder or crippling injury is imminent, but do I have to *wait* until I know I'm going to be killed to stop someone who is hassling me? No! I need to use a lesser level of force to get a few seconds to escape *before* the situation becomes lethal.

In a gun-phobic society, we are encountering more and more places where the law prohibits carrying a firearm. Leaving the issue of the

Just because you're knocked to the ground doesn't mean you've lost the fight. Learn to move, kick and trap from the ground so you can survive this common assault tactic.

constitutionality of these bans, we must talk about intermediate weapons to carry from your car into the courtroom, from the parking lot into the post office and other restricted areas.

Aerosol defense

Pepper spray, the aerosol deterrent that has all but replaced Mace®, is one of the most commonly carried deterrent sprays. Formally called Oleoresin Capsicum (OC), the oil of the red pepper disables most assailants, failing when not enough is used or when the wind blows the pepper spray away from the target. According to a 1993 article in *Law Enforcement Technology* magazine, the New Britain, Connecticut police department has 360 documented episodes of OC use over two-and-a-half years. They cite a 95% effectiveness rate for that period.

The best thing about OC, compared to earlier chemical restraint agents, is its proven effectiveness against drug influenced, intoxicated, deranged, and enraged individuals. The material is currently in use as a grizzly bear deterrent, and is also extremely effective against dogs. Only strictly trained attack dogs have been shown to withstand an application of pepper spray.

What the experts say

Between 1987 and 1989, the Federal Bureau of Investigation studied and tested pepper sprays. In one report, the FBI showed that virtually 100% of the 59 people sprayed suffered inflammation of mucous membranes and upper respiratory systems. Breathing the pepper spray caused coughing, shortness of breath, gasping, and a gagging sensation in the throat. Eyes close involuntarily as the OC comes in contact with the sensitive tissue. Skin inflammation is common, ranging from redness to acute burning. Perspiring or fair-skinned people suffer greater skin discomfort. Some lose upper body motor skills for a short time.

FBI results confirmed information coming out of police reports about OC: success depended on discharging enough OC at the target. They suggested at least one three-second burst or three one-second bursts.

Their tests showed the OC is more effective in enclosed areas, like buildings and rooms. I would add that you need to be aware that wind will disperse OC spray if it is used outdoors. On the other hand, you need to get out of the area yourself after discharging OC into the air, so you don't inhale the agent.

Interestingly, during the FBI's evaluation, none of their spray test subjects required medical attention. In 1993, the first reported death after police use of OC occurred after a subject with respiratory problems was subdued with OC. Civilians carrying the product on the street should be ready to retreat after spraying, then call 911 to report the incident and request professional assistance for the person sprayed. The sprayed assailant may need protection from threats like automobiles in the street. Engaging bystanders to stop traffic if the sprayed assailant wanders into the street would be a reasonable, responsible effort. After any act of self defense, report the incident to protect yourself from prosecution by your attacker, and to establish a record of the attack in case you must later prove a pattern of harassment.

Varied reports, including my own experience show that coughing and respiratory discomfort generally ends fifteen to twenty minutes after fresh, uncontaminated air is available. Skin irritation may well linger for half an hour or more. The best antidote for OC spray is soap and cold water to remove it from skin, and plenty of cool, running water to bathe the eyes. Generally, the effects of contact with OC spray will disappear in 30 to 45 minutes.

Spray selection

OC spray is marketed in varying intensities, ranging from 5% OC in a base carrier to 10% OC. While a higher percentage may be preferable, my experience and observations from the "receiving end" indicate that 5% is fully effective. In selecting an OC spray for intermediate defense, I would advise more concern about the delivery system. OC spray manufacturers have marketed two delivery systems: an aerosol spray that comes out of the container in a cone-shaped cloud and cans that deliver a steady stream.

For civilian self defense, our instructor trainers have recommended the cone-shaped aerosol delivery, and I concur. Your intermediate defense goal is escape, after temporarily disabling the assailant. The stream delivery system affects the area hit, but is more difficult to deliver to the eyes, nose or mouth, since it is only a thin stream. The cone-shaped cloud, however, mists out from the container and is impossible to keep out of the nose and lungs. The mist settles on the skin and causes irritation, as well.

The author recommends and carries oleoresin capsicum as an intermediate defensive tool, since it allows the defender to maintain distance from the assailant.

Against experienced subjects intent on holding their breath, deliver the mist in three or more one-second blasts. For example, you are crossing a crowded supermarket parking lot when a deranged person rushes at you, fists clenched, face distorted. "Get back! Don't come any closer," you yell in a commanding voice. The OC spray is in your hand, and you have it up and ready to spray. Your non-dominant arm is fully extended to deflect the assailant. If they don't obey your command, you discharge the spray in short, repeated bursts.

A determined attacker will not go down immediately. Multiple attackers will require greater quantities of OC spray. Wind makes it more difficult to get the OC into the attacker's face right away, and will require a number of bursts to get the job done. All of these circumstances lead me to advise carrying at least 1.5 to 2 ounces of spray, more than the little key-ring cannisters contain.

After breathing or contacting the mist, the assailant is likely to go to their knees. When in pain and blinded, it's a natural instinctive motion to bring the hands to the face and double over. At this moment, chose the nearest escape--return to the store or get into your car. Call 911 as soon as possible to report the attempted assault and your response. The assailant may need help during the next half hour as they recover from the effects of the pepper spray. This is not your duty, but the job of police or paramedics.

Few weapons can instantaneously stop an assault. OC is no different. Though the results are impressive, tests and my own experience show that the person sprayed is capable of continued forward movement for several seconds after fully contacting the OC mist. To avoid being stabbed, stricken or otherwise assaulted, you need to spray and move away at a 90° angle from the attacker. Always disengage and run for cover. Don't mistakenly believe that OC is the magic formula that will fully protect you.

If you use the OC canister you carry, replace it after the incident to be sure you have a sufficient quantity if you ever need it again. When you buy a new canister, give it a brief test spray to be sure the nozzle is functional. You should continue to test the canister every four to six months to be sure the aerosol propellant has not escaped or the nozzle hasn't become clogged.

OC sprays are illegal on commercial airlines, and your canister will be confiscated if you attempt to take it through with carry-on baggage. At publication time, nine states restrict purchase, carry and use of OC sprays. Many have incorrectly classified the aerosol agent as a "tear gas." Restrictions range from age limits for purchase to a licensing requirement, much like concealed carry permits for handguns. Other states, like New York and Washington, D.C. strictly prohibit its use. Violations can result in charges ranging from misdemeanors to felony charges. Before carrying OC spray, especially if you bought it outside the area you wish to carry it in, call the local law enforcement agency and ask about laws concerning its use and possession.

Pepper spray sounds like a wonderful defense tool, doesn't it? I certainly like having it among my defenses, but please *do not make the mistake of believing it is more effective than it really is.* A spray won't do the job in high wind or at great distances. It takes longer to affect a person wearing a baseball cap and wrap-around sunglasses. The old saying could be updated to: Don't bring a spray to a gun fight. Aerosol restraint sprays, empty hand techniques, and other intermediate weapons are in your hands to buy you the seconds needed to escape or draw your gun. If the assailant has grabbed you, they will be able to hang on and harm you even after taking a full dose of OC. Be ready with an alternative defense. Don't rely entirely on the spray!

"What is that stick on your key chain?"

Any intermediate weapon is useful only if it is *in your hand*. During the show I spoke of at the beginning of this chapter, a few women came up and smugly showed me the small OC canister in their handbag. "That's good," I encouraged, "but you ought to start carrying it in your hand. Don't fool yourself into thinking you can guess when trouble will strike."

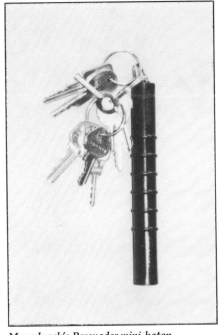

Monadnock's Persuader mini-baton.

73

The intermediate weapon most natural to carry continuously is the mini-baton. It attaches to the key chain, and at 5 1/2" long by 5/8" diameter, it fits naturally into the hand. The mini-baton was developed

The author and LFI student Karl Wingren show use of the Persuader to escape a rear grab.

in the 1950s by Takayuki Kubota for California businessmen needing a defensive art. Looking for items the businessmen carried regularly, he developed a defense system using writing pens. The pen was later replaced with the metal or plastic mini-baton we know today. The Kubotan has grooves to keep it from slipping in the defender's hand and to help it stay in position on the assailant during squeezing or leveraging techniques.

The Monadnock Company produces a mini-baton called the "Persuader." Of identical dimensions to the Kubotan, the Persuader is also available with ridges that contact the nerve and bone during certain techniques.

Neither version of the mini-baton is of great value without appropriate training. Persuader techniques are based on an understanding of nerve and pressure points. Pressed or jabbed into these points, the baton causes sharp pain that distracts the assailant. As he loosens his grip or hesitates momentarily, the defender escapes. Kubotan techniques rely on pain compliance. Applied properly to the wrist, the mini-baton is used to remove an assailant who is grabbing the front of your clothing, and drive him to the ground. Grabs from behind are countered by driving the end of the baton into the delicate bones on the back of the hand or into selected points on the arm.

Because leverage and pain compliance are at the heart of mini-baton techniques, size disparity is not a disadvantage to the petite mini-baton user. However, in teaching Persuader techniques, the Firearms Academy of Seattle staff has encountered a few students with very high pain tolerances, who exhibit little response to the pain compliance techniques. It is reasonable to expect that as many as one in fifteen people can endure this level of pain, so we must be prepared to switch to another kind of defensive tactic if the technique, properly applied, fails to elicit an immediate response. Remain fluid: if the pain compliance approach doesn't work, quickly switch to a destroying technique.

Mini-baton training also includes jabs and flaying with the keys on the end of the baton that can inflict a high level of pain and damage, depending on the location of the blow.

Facing the blade

I'd prefer a long impact weapon over the Persuader if I had to face a knife when not carrying a gun. If a gun was not available, an expandable baton or police-style flashlight offers some help. Research by Dennis Tueller of Salt Lake City Police proved conclusively that knifers

Without large obstacles as protection against a rushing assault, an assailant can stab you before you can ever draw your gun.

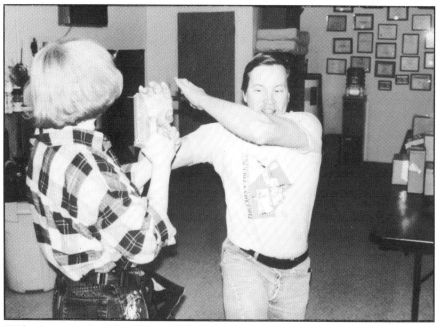

Without cover, an "assailant" can stab the author at about the same time as her dummy gun, drawn from a fanny pack, can fire one round.

can dash up to 21 feet in less than the two seconds it takes a skilled handgunner to draw and fire two shots into the assailant. The Tueller study taught us several additional lessons: to maintain an extreme distance from those posing a threat, the importance of moving on a 90°

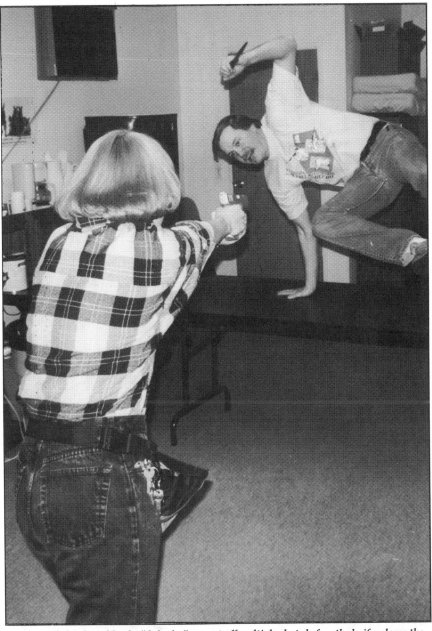

Retreating behind a table, the "defender" can get off multiple shots before the knifer clears the obstacle and is within contact distance.

line out of the path of a charging attacker, and the absolute and deadly danger of contact weapons.

Distance equals survival in a knife fight. Defenses that create distance between you and the knife-wielding assailant give you time to draw a gun or escape. A four-cell impact flashlight or an expandable baton extends your reach twelve to twenty inches, distancing you from the knife, and giving you a striking weapon to bash into the offender. Courses in baton use ingrain skills that the trained individual can use with an improvised weapon—a stick or a garden tool handle. Don't bypass training and go right to the security guard supply store to buy a baton or flashlight. Impact weapons can be grabbed and used viciously against you if you jab or stick the weapon at the assailant. Lightning fast strikes are more difficult to dodge, and impossible for the assailant to harmlessly catch the weapon and take it away. Integral to this kind of training is the footwork to keep you in position to cause harm, but out of the way of retaliatory strikes, slashes or kicks.

Calibre Press has produced a video *Surviving Edged Weapons* that is must-see viewing for anyone at risk from knife-armed assailants.[1]

A heavy Maglight flashlight can serve as a weapon in an emergency.

Lies and dangerous scams

In a society that does not trust women with deadly force, we are often given ineffective, dangerous tools for our defense.

"#1 Police Recommended Safety Device." Funny, I read that claim on an ad for a stun gun, and less than a week later, was told by a high-decibel personal alarm saleswoman that *their* device was the #1 police recommended safety device! The truth is that neither is adequate defense in an attack. The stun gun, with advertisers bragging about 75,000-volt shocks, works only if both terminals are held against the attacker for seven to ten seconds, until the muscles go into spasm. No one, not even a small person, will compliantly stand still while you hold the stun gun against them. A struggle will break the contact before the muscle spasm can be induced. *Why are women being told to use non-lethal gimmicks against rape and lethal assault?*

High-decibel noisemakers are being touted as deterrents to assault. The high-pitched siren "will drive him away and bring help," say the promoters. These devices sound much like car alarms. The sirens on car alarms are now considered more of a nuisance than a deterrent. If the

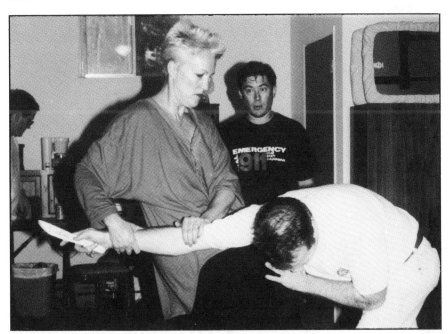

FAS student Terry Hollis practices knife defenses against fellow student Brady Wright. Visiting instructor Clyde Caceres supervises the exercise.

owner is in hearing range, he or she can run to the car to quiet the alarm, but no one, police or otherwise, responds to the squeal of a car alarm. Do not believe noisemaker claims that a siren will summon help. It will not.

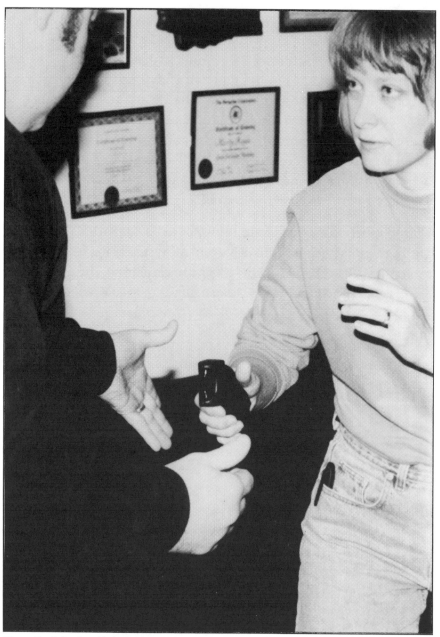

The author's husband helps in a demonstration showing the ineffectiveness of the stun gun. Here he closes in, receiving a brief electric shock...

I *do* like the motion-sensing noisemakers as budget alarm systems, if you can adjust the device so it responds only to gross movement, like the opening of a door or window. Not everyone can afford to pay a major company to install an alarm system, but all of us need ways to be sure our doors and windows won't be pried open as we sleep, allowing an intruder in our homes while we are vulnerable. Attach one to your sliding patio door or to windows that don't have adequate locks.

Tools are only as good as your training

Any self defense device is only as useful as the training you receive in its use. Even the simple OC spray has specific techniques that make it more effective. Equally important is the legal defense you muster by presenting training certificates in both non-lethal and firearms defensive techniques. Your training certificates tell the prosecutor, judge and jury that you carefully trained to stop varying levels of criminal behavior. You can tell the court that your training and preparation was the basis for the method with which you choose to defend yourself and your family.

Legitimate instructors of the mini-baton, oleoresin capsicum, stick fighting, or hand-to-hand defenses *must* inform you that intermediate

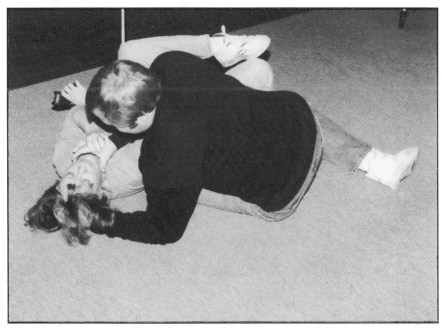

...and throws the author to the ground simulating an attack.

force is not sufficient against a deadly force attack. Use intermediate defenses to stop harassment *before* a lethal assault begins, but always be prepared to answer lethal force with your own firearm if that is the kind of attack you face.

---

[1] *Surviving Edged Weapons*, Calibre Press, Inc., 666 Dundee Rd., St. 1607, Northbrook, ILL 60062-2727 (800) 323-0037.

9
Rape Survival

If we are to stop sexual assault, we need to understand what motivates the rapist, what can be done to survive *during* a sexual assault and what to do after a rape. While we train to prevent sexual violence, it would be foolish to conclude that we are now invulnerable to this threat. This chapter incorporates information presented in newsletters and brochures made available by the American Women's Self Defense Association, an organization to which I proudly belong.[1]

Understanding rape

The rapist's goal is violent control over another human being. Some rapists need to degrade their victim, others want to see the terror their acts cause. For others, the ultimate control of life or death is the key to their satisfaction.

Statistics reveal that women often know the rapist. Don't assume you are safe because you know an individual from work, from social or church contacts, or from your family. The Biden report states "Strangers are not the most dangerous sources of violence against women. The numbers of women attacked by those they loved, those they had just met, far outweighed the number of women attacked by strangers."[2]

Too many women have obtained a court order restraining a male offender from further contact with her or her children, only to find that the restraining order was useful only in pressing further legal action, and of no use whatsoever in assuring her safety. If a spouse, boyfriend or acquaintance harasses or assaults you, the responsibility will rest on you to defend yourself. The police simply cannot arrive in time to stop a determined attacker.

Restraining orders *are*, however, useful in pressing further charges against an abuser. The victim needs to file police reports and keep scrupulously truthful records of restraining order violations, listing dates, times, and descriptions of the incident. Write down your response to the abuser and list any witnesses who can corroborate your testimony.

Rape prevention

The quality of your training will keep you alive. Assault and rape prevention training includes physical fighting skills, weapons use, and panic control. Your training will help you keep a level head, because you *know* what to do in advance. Expect to feel the fear, but remember that you have been trained and know how to protect yourself. Use your mind to stop the panic.

Don't expect to be saved by pleading, stalling, reasoning or crying. Remember that the rapist rapes to control and degrade his victim, not for sexual gratification. Establish your refusal to be a victim. Take the first opportunity to resist and escape. Use any object available—a bedside lamp, the corner of a hard-bound book, a stone or object picked off the street—to smash an attacker's face, nose and eyes, Adam's apple, knee or groin.

Look for a way to escape immediately. Many women escape a threatened rape by running and screaming. Statistics show that a combination of forceful verbal commands and physical resistance, including escape, provide the greatest chance of stopping a sexual assault. Be prepared to support your verbal and physical resistance with a weapon appropriate to the force used against you.

Rape is a deadly force attack. Sometimes the rapist uses verbal threats and implied threat by his greater physical size and strength. Although a knife may not be at your throat, non-consensual intercourse is still a lethal attack *because of the implication that he will use any degree of force necessary to gain your compliance.* Too often men trivialize the issue of rape by saying that no one was ever killed by a penis or mockingly advise the victim to relax and enjoy the rape. This kind of insensitivity discourages women from understanding that they can use deadly force against a rapist because it is his threat of death or crippling injury that causes the victim to submit to non-consensual intercourse, not the threat of the sexual act itself.

You may face an unarmed assailant who uses his greater strength and size to coerce and gain cooperation. Assailants did not use a gun in

89.6% of the violent crimes against women between 1973 and 1983. During that same time, only 10% of the reported rapists employed a gun.[3]

Understand, however, that you can resist an armed rapist. Knives are frequently used, but prior training can help you survive against a knife. People are usually cut during a knife assault, but survival *is* possible. Be prepared to be cut and to bleed, but keep fighting to gain your freedom. With proper training, you can disarm a gun-carrying assailant, as well.

Early resistance can prevent life-threatening danger after the rape. Don't allow yourself to be tied up. The vast majority of victims who are restrained are murdered during the assault. It is better to fight for your life while you can resist, than to leave your survival in the hands of your assailant.

For decades, women have been warned not to resist rape, counseled by men and agencies who understood neither the effects of rape on the victim, nor the motivation of the rapist. This is, and has always been, a *lie*. Refuse to believe anyone who does not value your life and survival.

Citing National Crime Survey data gathered after 1978, author Don Kates reports, "The gun-armed resister was actually much less likely to be injured than the non resister who was, in turn, much less likely to be injured than those who resisted without a gun. Only 12 to 17 percent of gun-armed resisters were injured. Those who submitted to the felons' demands were twice as likely to be injured (gratuitously [after the rape or incident]). Those resisting without guns were three times as likely to be injured as those with guns."[4]

No one can teach you specific sets of movements to stop a rapist, since each attack is unique. Learn principles of defense. When under attack, move rapidly and assertively. Think clearly. Don't panic. Do the best you can with the tools you have, even if that is only your empty hands.

If you are raped

Avoid panic. If the rapist prevails try to remain aware of his actions and alert to escape possibilities during the assault. Never decide that you are defeated. Never give up. With increasing frequency, rapists are killing their victims to avoid arrest or for their own satisfaction. Do not consider the attack over until the rapist is truly gone.

A certified handgun retention instructor can teach techniques to counter the fear that your gun will be taken and used against you. Here, petite DeAnne Orive proves that Jim Lindell's retention system works, even if the attacker is much larger, as is fellow-student Dan Beacon.

Try to remember the details of the assault. You will be enduring the most difficult time of your life, but it is important to cooperate with authorities so they can help you and stop the rapist before he strikes again. Always report any rape or any attempted rape to the police.

Notice details about the assailant, guess his height and weight; take note of what he is wearing. Look for distinctive physical characteristics like a muscular or thin physique, his complexion, tatoos, scars or blemishes, hair and eye color. Try to see the direction in which he leaves. If he uses a car, try to determine make, model and year, and remember some of the license number and state. If you can't determine the make of the car, try to remember the emblem on the car well enough to draw it for an investigator. Leave your fingerprints everywhere you possibly can, drop personal items that can be identified as yours, including buttons, jewelry, gloves or cosmetic cases with your fingerprints.

Afterwards, do not bathe, change or wash clothing. Don't clean your nails or apply medication. Your body holds important evidence that will be used in prosecuting the attacker.

Call the police immediately. The police need to conduct a thorough investigation of the crime and the place it happened. Although it will be difficult for you to recount, the investigators need to discuss the assault in detail. Your help is needed to stop the rapist from hurting you and others any more. A friend can accompany you to a hospital for examinations and tests. If you want a female law enforcement officer, ask the investigators if one is available. Many cities have rape crisis centers. They can provide counseling and help you find legal advice.

Don't be dissuaded from pressing charges. Rapists often threaten to return if you report the assault or press charges. Only your testimony can stop the rapist. Your testimony reduces the chance that the rapist will do the same violence to someone else.

[1] American Women's Self Defense Association, 713 N. Wellwood Ave., Lindenhurst, NY 11757.

[2] *Violence Against Women: A Week in the Life of America,* A majority staff report prepared for the Committee on the Judiciary, United States Senate, 102nd Congress, 2nd Session. Oct. 1992.

[3,4] Kates, Don B., *Guns, Murder and the Constitution,* 1991.

10
Staying Safe

As girls we are taught behavior that keeps us from taking responsibility for our own well-being. We're taught to look to others to protect us, and we're taught not to fight. By the time we're teenagers, we'd rather die or be harmed than disobey the taboo of fighting back. The tenets of religion somehow get distorted and we think it's wrong to hurt another in our own defense. Other distortions place the survival of each individual in God's hands. Because scripture says "He sees the sparrow fall," some believe God will decide if they should enjoy safety or become a victim. Had God wanted that kind of dependency, we would have been given animal minds, not reasoning ability. When evil happens, some say, "It must have been God's will..." Or might it have been our own irresponsibility?

Please hear this: **It's OK to fight.** Clear up any confusion by understanding that it's OK to fight for your *life*, although you should not kill in defense of your material possessions.

Feminine irresponsibility is demonstrated in the desire to remain child-like and carefree—the Peter Pan mindset. Carelessness is like a drug, it gives a euphoria, and those hooked on it have a hard time accepting the reality of this risky world. I remember practicing carelessness in my twenties, drinking with my friends and taking stupid chances. By way of confession, let me say that it is a credit to the friends looking out for me that I came through those reckless years unscathed. I remember friends pulling me out of barroom situations, walking me home, and making otherwise, protective gestures. In the last decade, society has changed the way it looks at social behavior. A lot of us used to go out drinking, then drive ourselves home. Today, few of us will challenge the rule such interdicts that behavior. Why aren't we willing to accept that it is dangerous to be in Condition White in public places, just as we are willing to accept that we are in danger if we drive ourselves home after a night of drinking? When partying, appoint a designated caretaker. If you go to clubs and bars, take along someone who will remain sober and keep you from leaving with strangers. Promise to honor that person's word, the same way you would hand over the car keys to a designated driver.

Thought this was going to be a book all about guns, didn't you? Well, we'll get into that next, but it is terribly important that gun owners be mature enough to handle the responsibility of immediate access to the power of life and death. Your daily decisions about how you live reveal your attitude toward life and death! First, address your delusions and mental blocks that *put* you in danger, then learn the skills to protect yourself.

Taking this level of personal responsibility is really about caring enough for yourself to assure your own survival. If you don't care enough about yourself, maybe you care enough about those who love you—a child your death would orphan, a lover your death would widow, a parent left alone in old age. Your awareness and self-responsibility can spare them the anguish of dealing with a loved one's horrible death.

Finally, if you don't care enough about those who love you, can you find it in yourself to care enough about the world we are creating for those who follow us? Will it be a world where assault and victimization is a quasi-acceptable thing, like forgery or embezzlement, or will it be shaped by women who have stood up and said *no more*—then taken the steps to make it a safer world?

11
Safe Gun Habits to Live By

"I was told the gun is unloaded, so I don't have to be careful with it."

Uncounted firearms tragedies are "explained" by people who believed the gun was not loaded. You can save yourself this sorrow if you *always treat every gun as if it is loaded*...even if you just laid it down or if someone hands it to you and says, "It's OK, it's not loaded."

In a gun store or shooting range, check any gun you are handed to determine that it is indeed unloaded. Learn to check for ammunition in the gun by both sight and feel. Some semi-automatic pistols have chambers that are obscured by the slide even when locked open. A round of ammunition may be hidden in the chamber, ready to fire if the trigger is pulled. A probing finger can detect the presence of a cartridge you cannot see. Training yourself to verify an empty gun by sight and

A visual and tactile check of the chamber ensures that the gun is truly empty.

91

feel prepares you to unload a weapon safely after a night-time emergency.

We don't have the room to go into unloading different types of weapons in this book, that's a topic for a following volume. Ask a knowledgeable gun store clerk or an experienced shooter to show you how to safely unload your revolver or a semi-automatic.

Safe gun handling demands that you *never point the gun at anything you would not shoot.* The rule applies equally to both loaded and unloaded guns. Always know what and who the gun muzzle will cross. And remember, a visual barrier, like a sheet rock wall, will not stop bullets. Determine a safe muzzle direction *before* picking up the weapon, that way you won't cross your self or someone else with the muzzle while you look for a safe place to point it. Avoid handling firearms off the range unless you are safely practicing dry fire, cleaning the gun, or securing it for the night. Don't show off the gun like a toy or curiosity. Treat your personal protection weapon as a very private item, much like your lingerie or cosmetics.

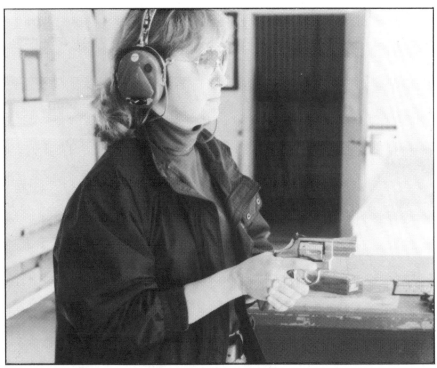

The trigger finger stays OUTSIDE the trigger guard until the target is behind your sights and you are ready to shoot.

Maintain gun safety habits always

Treat every gun as if it is loaded; never point a gun at anything you are not willing to shoot. These are the first rules of safe gun handling. The third rule, *keep your finger outside the trigger guard until your sights are on target* is equally important. As we go on to discuss tactics and concerns of people who face an assailant or intruder, we'll refer to the startle response or sympathetic interlimb response.

Suppose you hear noises in the kitchen some night. Gun in hand, you go downstairs to investigate. As you approach, the noises continue. You are convinced you will soon face a dangerous intruder. In the grip of this stress and fear, *anything* that moves will startle you, and your body will contract and tighten, entering its natural fight-or-flight condition.

If anything startles you now, your hands and arms automatically convulse. Your grip on the handgun becomes a death grip. When the fingers gripping the handgun tighten, the trigger finger will automatically contract, too. If the finger rests on the trigger, the trigger will be pulled. On a single-action semi-auto, this pretty much guarantees that an unintentional shot will be fired. A revolver or double action semi-auto can also be fired, depending on the severity of the startle response.

In more ordinary day-to-day circumstances, keeping the finger off the trigger avoids almost all the negligent gun accidents that can happen, because guns don't just go off by themselves. Someone has to pull the trigger.

Never break the rules because you know the gun is unloaded. Your actions are the basis for habits that will be repeated under circumstances that are **not** safe.

Safe shooting locations

One of life's ironies is the danger of shooting in many of the informal public shooting areas. All across the country, in timber land and other remote areas, the public is allowed to discharge firearms. The danger of shooting in remote, isolated areas comes from thieves and marauders who recognize the vulnerability of small groups or lone shooters. The solitary individual is lulled into complacency by conversation with a couple of strangers who purport to be fellow shooters, coming to use the firing area. When our good-gal's guard is down, the predator restrains them and steals the firearms. Women are also at risk of sexual attack, having been disarmed by the robbers.

Personal safety sometimes costs a little more. Spend the $50 to join a local rifle and pistol club, or rent a lane at an indoor gun club where a range safety officer is present at all times. Shooting in isolated areas is a dangerous activity, not only because of thieves, but because of the unsafe activities of weekend warriors.

Informal outdoor shooting areas pose great peril to hikers, dirt bikers or wandering children who may pop up over your backstop. When you fire your gun, you must know that your target is safe to shoot at, as well as being certain what is behind that target. This safety rule is probably the strongest argument against shooting on an unorganized range.

Even if you shoot at an indoor range, take responsibility to keep the range safe while you are there. Don't be afraid to correct unsafe gun handling by others or notify the range safety officer. If you complain that guns have been pointed your direction, and the offense continues, leave the range. People become over-stimulated while shooting, and just because they state the weapon is unloaded is no guarantee that they

An organized shooting club or supervised public range is a safer practice environment than forest land or gravel pits.

haven't removed the magazine, but forgotten to take the round out of the chamber.

Protect your senses

Avoiding being shot is not your only safety concern on a firing range. You have to take care of your hearing and vision, both of which may be damaged during firearms discharge. Repeated exposure to loud noises has robbed a lot of shooters of their hearing. At a minimum, use the foam protectors inserted into the ear to block the noise. Good quality ear muffs are the better choice, since they block more of the noise. Muffs also cover the sound-conducting bones around the ear that can transmit damagingly loud concussions during gun fire. A lot of beginning shooters display an exaggerated flinching reaction when their handgun fires. There are several reasons for the flinch, which we'll discuss later. One aspect is anticipation of the painfully loud noise. That's avoidable with a $20 to $30 purchase of ear muffs.

Equally important is eye protection. Shooting a semi-automatic, or shooting beside someone with a semi-automatic, you quickly realize that the bullet isn't the only object being thrown around. The empty

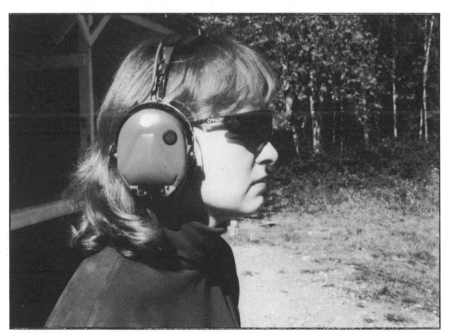

For good eye and ear protection, the author favors the amplified Wolf's Ears and a pair of Oakley Blades.

95

case being extracted from the semi-auto jumps out of the gun with enough force to cause serious injury if it strikes the eye.

Flying brass cartridge cases are a common danger. Less common, but posing a much greater danger, is the possibility that an ammunition cartridge may be faulty and blow apart the gun. If this happens, metal shards are exploded in every direction. In other instances, the gun itself malfunctions, and an unlocked breach at the moment the cartridge is detonated allows parts of the brass case to break out and fly in all directions like a little grenade. Both are sobering accidents, and can blind vulnerable eyes without adequate protection.

Buy eye glasses designed as protection against firearms accidents, not just sunglasses. The polycarbonate material needs to meet or exceed the ANSI Z 87.1 Industrial Standards for impact resistance. Do not trust your drug store sunglasses to do the job!

Be sure the ammunition and gun are the same caliber

Be careful that the ammunition you buy is the correct caliber for your firearm. The gun's construction is designed to be strong enough to withstand the pressures of the round it is designed to fire. Some ammunition-gun misfits are self-diagnosing. The powerful .357 magnum cartridge is identical in diameter to the .38 Special cartridge. It cannot be fired in a .38 caliber handgun because it is slightly longer, and the .38's cylinder can't close with .357 cartridges inside. Smaller cartridges will fit in the chamber of a larger caliber gun, but dangers include malfunctions that happen when the case doesn't eject from a semi auto, as well as bursting the cartridge's case wall if it expands when the powder is burning.

You can be certain you've purchased the correct ammunition, if the caliber shown on the box corresponds with the caliber stamped into the frame or barrel of your handgun. If you're not sure you have the right caliber of ammunition, ask a knowledgeable gun store clerk for advice.

If you own several handguns of different calibers, only fire one at a time when you're at the range. Set out the .380 ACP and its ammunition. When you're done firing the little gun, bring out the 9mm semi-auto, but don't have both guns and both calibers of ammunition on the line at the same time.

12
Basic Training

While there may exist a few naturally talented shooters, accurate shooting skill is not a genetic ability. Marksmanship is the result of a specific set of psycho-motor skills that adults can learn and maintain. For example, an experienced, trained shooter manipulates the trigger with a finger that is acting in disassociation from the other muscles of the hand. The untrained finger convulses as the hands tighten on the gun in anticipation of the shots and recoil. That inadvertent motion on the trigger pulls the shot off center. You need to *know* you can reliably place your gunshots where needed, avoiding misses and endangering innocent bystanders.

The question of how much marksmanship training is enough varies from individual to individual, but I believe anyone who carries a handgun for defense needs to study and practice tactical drills that

Author works with woman student at a Lethal Force Institute class held near Seattle.

require split-second decision making, as well as practicing accurate shot placement. These skills far exceed being able to place five shots *at your leisure* in the X ring of a paper target!

Don't ask a male friend or lover to teach you to shoot. A man can become a decent shooter without adopting a technically correct shooting stance, because the mass and strength in his upper body controls the recoil better. The female physique typically has much less upper body mass to absorb the handgun's recoil. A woman's legs are her stronger limbs and she can position her body to take advantage of this strength. Women's smaller, thinner hands grip the gun and manipulate the trigger differently. Despite his good intentions, even a master of tactical skills—a policeman or member of the armed forces—cannot intuit the female body's response to firing a handgun.

The intimidating task of learning to defend oneself with a deadly weapon is a job better approached without the emotional baggage of a relationship. At this point, you need a respected teacher, not a beloved friend. Self defense issues that have nothing to do with shooting ability also need to be addressed. Women will have different concerns, and, to some degree, different parameters governing their use of deadly force. A classroom format that allows you to learn with other women or with women *and* men, should offer a forum to discuss female-specific issues in self defense and in shooting.

Take time to find a training course that is sensitive to women's concerns about self defense. Check the phone directory for a list of firearm or handgun instructors, or start by calling or visiting the gun shops and commercial shooting ranges in your area. Ask for names of people in the area who offer beginning defensive handgun instruction.

After compiling a list of likely candidates, contact these instructors and ask for a résumé of their credentials. Ask about their philosophy of women's self defense, who they trained with, the length of their experience as an instructor, if they participate in competitive shooting events, and what their attitude is toward women shooters. Get to know the mindset of your potential instructor. Ask if they discuss local handgun laws and use of deadly force, in addition to their range instruction. Ask for a brief written course description for their beginning shooting classes. An excellent starting place is a handgun safety seminar or an introduction to handguns. An inexpensive one-day or evening course gives you a chance to decide if you like the instructor's teaching style and to learn about other courses.

The Weaver shooting stance works well for men like Phil Steinert, a Marine firearms instructor, who has strong arms and upper body. Women, however, generally shoot better in the aggressive Isosceles stance shown by the author, since it relies less on upper body strength.

What to look for

A basic defensive firearms course should include an awful lot more than learning to shoot accurately. Is the world's best target-shooter prepared to save their own life if they are not truly convinced of their right to use the firearm to stop a violent assault? Many questions arise about appropriate use of deadly force—is it OK to shoot someone who is running out of your house with your jewelry and television? If you can't find an instructor who includes material on the use of deadly force in their curriculum, obtain and read Massad Ayoob's *In the Gravest Extreme*. At the very least educate yourself about your responsibility as an armed citizen by visiting the law library at your county courthouse to read up on your area's firearms-related law.

Next—I believe a basic handgun course should provide beginning students with appropriate training guns and ammunition. First-time shooters learn the fundamentals of marksmanship most easily with the "friendly" .22 caliber revolver and semi-automatic. After becoming safe and proficient with a training gun, the student can move on to a caliber that is big enough for self defense. A lot of beginners can avoid purchasing a gun that's not right for them by joining a friendly, low-key class with the handguns and ammunition already supplied. They learn to shoot, they have the chance to ask lots of questions about handguns and defensive ammunition, concealed carry, safety, care and maintenance and cleaning of the weapons, *before* dealing with the expense and confusion of their first gun purchase.

Professional training is a "must" before adopting the gun for self defense. If you absolutely cannot find competent training in your area, arrangements can be made for qualified instructors to come to your area.[1]

When beginning training is complete and those questions answered, the student is able to present herself knowledgeably at a gun counter and fend off the patronizing suggestions that the little lady needs a pretty little gun—maybe this .25 caliber Raven here in the bottom shelf. The woman can respond that she would prefer, perhaps, that nice S & W 3913, and ask "may I see it please, sir?"

Next, buying a gun for self defense.

---

[1] If you are interested in hosting a course by the author in your area, call The Firearms Academy of Seattle, (800) 327-2666.

13
Annie, Get Your Gun

Shopping for a gun entails a lot more than finding a weapon that feels right in your hand. Though we will discuss guns that fit some hands better than others, the first-time gun owner must deal with other considerations, also.

When I asked Massad Ayoob what guns he recommended for women, he said it was a lot like asking a carpenter if you should buy a hammer or a saw. "What do you need to do with the tool?" he asked. A gun for home defense can be considerably larger than a gun for concealed carry. A person who can afford just one gun will have to consider its concealability beneath clothes for both hot and cold weather. Someone who can afford a summer gun and a winter gun, or a carry gun and

After completing a basic firearms class, a woman is better prepared to purchase a gun for self-defense.

a competition gun, must look for guns that locate features like the safety lever and magazine release in similar locations.

Gun vocabulary

Before heading out to the gun store, it helps to have a grasp of the terminology you will encounter. As illustrated, handguns are broken down into two basic categories: revolvers and semi-automatics.

The revolver is the simpler of the two. Modern double action revolvers fire when the trigger is pulled, drawing back and cocking the hammer. This same action moves the cylinder to line up a chamber (and cartridge if it is loaded) with the firing pin. At the end of the trigger pull the sear releases the hammer and lets it fall forward to strike the primer. On some revolvers the firing pin is integral to the hammer, and strikes the cartridge as described above. On other brands of revolvers, the hammer is flat and strikes a transfer bar which carries the impact to a spring loaded firing pin. Under the blow, the spring is overcome, and the firing pin jolts forward to hit the primer. When the primer is hit, its compound sparks, igniting the gunpowder.

Most handguns must be *cocked* to fire. A cocked hammer is one that has been drawn back or down, so there is some distance between it and the firing pin. Internally, drawing back the hammer lines up two parts, the hammer hook and the shelf of the sear. When they engage, the hammer will sit in the cocked position until light pressure on the trigger releases the sear from the hook and lets the hammer slam forward.

Cocking can be accomplished two ways—the shooter can manually pull the hammer back or the hammer can be cocked by the movement of the trigger, if the gun is of the double action variety. When the trigger is moved through the final 1/16th inch or so of its rearward travel, the hammer is released and slams forward to impact the firing pin or primer.

The semi-automatic handgun cocks the hammer one of two ways.

Initially, double action semi-automatics cock the hammer the same way as the revolver. A long trigger pull moves the hammer into a cocked position, then the end of the motion disconnects the sear from the hammer and allows the hammer to fall forward onto the firing pin. During subsequent shots, the slide's motion cocks the gun and the trigger pull is much shorter and lighter.

Single action semi-automatics must be cocked to fire, too, but the trigger cannot accomplish that task. A single action semi-automatic must be cocked when the slide is cycled to place ammunition in the chamber, or the shooter must manually cock the hammer. Every shot fires with the same pressure and length of trigger pull on a single action semi-automatic.

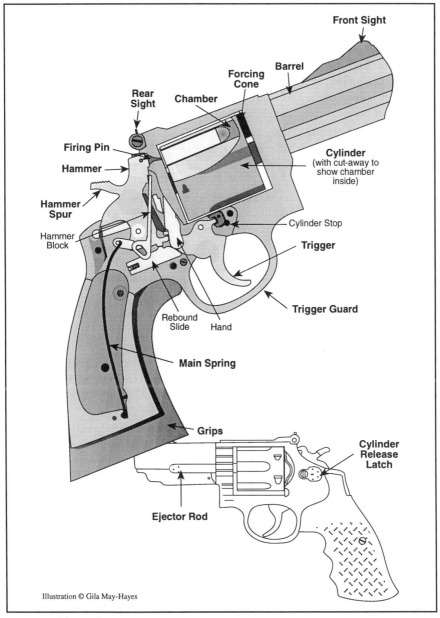

Illustration © Gila May-Hayes

Diagram of the revolver.

When the semi-automatic fires, the pressure generated by the burning gunpowder pushes the bullet out of the cartridge case and down the barrel. As the bullet leaves the end of the barrel, the pressure in the barrel and chamber sends the slide hurtling rearward, pushing down and cocking the hammer again. A small hook, the extractor, catches the

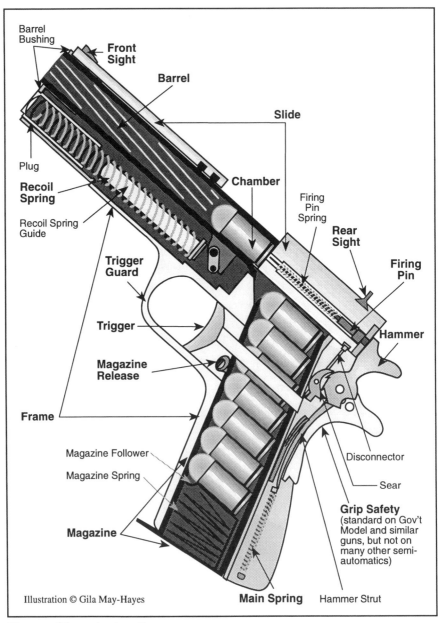

Diagram of the semi-automatic.

rim of the now-empty cartridge case and jerks it out of the chamber. As the empty case travels rearward, it strikes the ejector stud, and is flipped out of the ejection port that is cut in the slide of every semi-automatic.

When the slide reaches the end of its rearward travel, it is returned forward by the recoil spring, which was compressed when the slide flew to the rear. As the slide slams forward, it catches a fresh round of ammunition from the magazine and places it in the chamber. When the round is in the chamber, the slide locks with the barrel, putting the gun "into battery" and ready to fire another round.

After firing, the semi-automatic will be cocked. The safety of single action semi-automatics should be moved to the "on" position when the sights are not on target. A double action semi-automatic can be de-cocked—mechanically lowering the hammer safely and placing the trigger in the far-forward double-action position. The gun can then be carried with just the long trigger pull to keep the gun from being fired. Most double action semi-automatics also have a safety latch that can also be applied, locking the trigger for further safety.

The hammer spur on this Ruger SP101 has been removed, so it won't snag when it is drawn from beneath concealing garments. Nonetheless, the hammer's rearward travel is visible, as it moves down and back to a cocked position, driven by the shooter's pressure on the trigger. This is an example of shooting a revolver "double action."

In both revolvers and semi-automatics, we have a further division: double action guns, single action guns, and guns that operate double action only. In the most accurate, technical sense of the term, double action is a term used to describe a firearm that can be fired two ways— by manually cocking the hammer or by trigger cocking. With a double action, or trigger cocking gun, the trigger is pulled all the way from its most forward position to the rear, often as far as half an inch. The trigger movement draws back the hammer, preparing it to fall and strike the firing pin. To cock a single action gun, the hammer is held beneath the shooter's thumb and pulled down. As the thumb pulls the hammer down, the trigger moves to the rear, leaving only a short trigger pull, often about one-eighth inch, and the gun fires with very little pressure from the shooter's finger. Single-action semi-automatics are cocked by moving the slide to the rear, whether during the act of chambering a round or the slide's own movement during the firing cycle.

Common terminology deviates from the strictest technical use of the term "double action." While double action is generally used to describe trigger cocking, a Double Action Only (DAO) firearm is one that has *no*

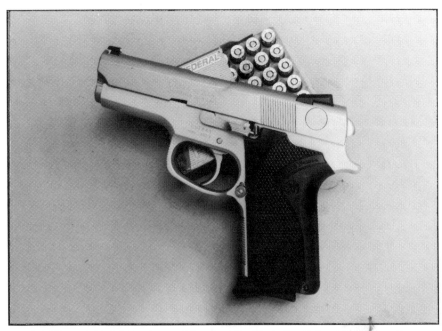

Smith & Wesson's Model 3953 is one of the nicest Double Action Only semi-autos on the market. To use informal gun lingo, both the S&W 3953 and the bobbed hammer Ruger on the previous page are double action only guns, since neither can be cocked. The correct technical expression would state that both are "trigger cocking" handguns.

provision for manual cocking—like a revolver with a bobbed or shrouded hammer. DAO revolvers include the Smith & Wesson Centennial lines, as well as revolvers with bobbed hammers, including Taurus' M85CH and Ruger's SP101 bobbed hammer variation. Double Action Only semi-autos are designed to return the trigger to the long, far-forward position after each shot. Double Action Only semi-autos are represented by Smith & Wesson's 3953, by Beretta's Model 92D, and by Ruger's P89 DAO.

Many modern semi-automatic pistols feature a decocking device that lets the owner safely take the firearm from single action to double action mode. The semi-auto will be slide-cocked, placed in single action mode after the slide has cycled, either from chambering the first round, or after firing. If the owner wants a double action trigger pull that requires a concerted effort to fire the gun (12 to 15 pounds of pressure), the hammer needs to be decocked. Examples of semi-automatics that can be manually decocked include the Ruger P91DC, Smith & Wesson 3913, the SIG semi-automatics, the Walther PPK, and Beretta and Taurus semi-autos. Some guns can be carried either decocked or on-safe. Left in single action, the safety can be applied; to fire single action the owner need merely sweep the safety off.

Finally, many semi-automatics have single action only triggers. The trigger is very short and requires only three to seven pounds pressure to cause the gun to fire. The hammer must be cocked for the gun to fire, either by racking the slide to chamber the round or by the slide's backward movement during the firing cycle. Examples of single action handguns include the Colt and Springfield Government Model 1911-style guns and their clones, as well as the Firestar semi-autos and Browning Hi Power handguns.

Stopping power: how big is big enough?

Before discussing gun choices, it must be reiterated that no handgun or ammunition is guaranteed to stop an assailant. Individuals have different abilities to withstand gunshot wounds. Self defense may require a number of shots to stop an assailant, especially if he is using drugs. Acknowledging that there is no magic gun or bullet, let's discuss the best choices available.

What follows is a breakdown of different styles and sizes of guns that the shopper can check out in her search for a self defense gun. Manufacturers are selected on perceived "staying power," an assumption that they will continue to provide quality handguns and service in the foreseeable future. This discussion of guns is by no means intended to be comprehensive, but is intended to give first-time buyers the terminology, concepts and considerations they need before laying down $200-600 on the counter of a gun shop.

When considering a handgun for self defense, a minimum should be the .38 caliber revolver loaded with at least +P ammunition. (See Ammunition, Chapter 15). A confrontation with an assailant is frightening enough without the disadvantage that a gun selected for small size and low recoil may not have the power to stop a deadly assault. Many believe the .380 ACP ammunition is powerful enough to stop an assailant, and indeed, stories are told in which the round performed admirably. People often choose the .380 because they want a small handgun they can conceal easily. The .380 semi-automatic ammunition has a small bullet and with a few notable exceptions, not many .380 semi-automatic handguns are enough smaller than the venerable .38 snubby revolver to justify the loss of velocity and bullet size.

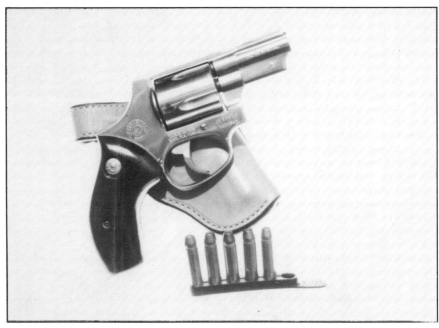

Taurus' excellent .38 Special revolver value: Model 85 CH, with the bobbed hammer, shown with Bianchi International's 55L holster for the bobbed-hammer gun.

Guns that chamber ammunition smaller than .380 ACP are *not* power-ful enough for use in self defense. Historically, .22 or .25 caliber guns have failed to stop assaults. The skull effectively shields the brain from this under-powered round, and the bullet doesn't carry enough energy to do much damage in body tissue, either. Probably the only hope for someone armed with a .25 caliber handgun is to try to penetrate the brain's medulla oblongata, but these kinds of shots are not usually possible in self defense situations.

People eventually die from small-caliber wounds, but death comes later from blood loss or infection. Your intention is to use a weapon of sufficient caliber to stop an assault. As a self defense shooter, your goal is not the death of the assailant, it is to put an immediate stop to hostile activity.

The .380 semi-automatic should be considered by people who have a condition that reduces hand strength, and *who will practice and train to become extremely accurate with their gun*. After one of our training courses, a student who suffers from arthritis chose a Beretta Model 86 .380 caliber semi-automatic. This gun's barrel tips up so the shooter can chamber the first round without having to manipulate the slide,

Beretta Model 86, with tip up barrel.

making it an excellent choice for people with physical conditions that affect hand strength. He has continued to practice and take classes, to ensure *beyond a shadow of a doubt* that he can deliver rapid, accurate fire in self defense.

The .380 semi-automatic is often carried as a back-up gun worn on the ankle or in a small shoulder holster as a second gun, insurance against malfunction or failure by a primary gun of larger caliber.

Revolver or semi-automatic

After stopping power, the most important consideration in gun selection is the amount of time you are willing to commit to training and maintenance. If you have little time to train, you will be better served by the revolver. If you are interested in shooting and can budget time for good training, frequent practice, and regular weapon maintenance you can benefit from the semi-automatic's ease of shooting.

Effective handgun selection requires truthful answers to several more questions. Does the buyer have sufficient upper body strength to work the slide of a semi-automatic gun? Willowy bodies with slender fingers

In double action, the big Taurus PT 101 AF doesn't fit the author's hands well enough for her to enjoy good marksmanship with the gun. Note that only the tip of her index finger contacts the trigger when the backstrap is centered in the web of her hand.

may find the slide of many semi-autos very difficult to manipulate. Remember, you have to manipulate the slide for a lot more than just unloading the gun. The slide has to be drawn back to chamber the first round, to clear malfunctions, and to take apart and clean the weapon after shooting practice. If it sounds like too much work, consider the user-friendly revolver.

It's pretty, but does it fit?

The buyer next needs to assure the proper fit of the gun in her hand. Could you drive a car with a non-adjustable seat that left you unable to fully depress the clutch? That question is no more absurd than asking if someone can shoot well with a gun that is too large for her hand. The index finger's distal joint needs to reach the trigger when the top of the backstrap or grip tang is centered in the web of the hand. It's nearly impossible to shoot a double action gun accurately with only the tip of the finger reaching the trigger.

Don't be fooled by gun salesmen who say, "just move your hand around until your finger reaches the trigger." The grip tang *needs* to be centered in the web of the hand so the trigger finger can pull straight back for accurate shooting. A fit that lets the grip tang ride against the

The author's medium sized hands fit the Government Model 1911-A1 semi-automatic .45 well.

111

thumb's base knuckle will transfer the recoil into the bony joint, resulting in poor recoil control, shooting discomfort, and eventual joint injury.

After assuring that the gun's backstrap-to-trigger measure fits your hand size, there are features that render some guns easier to shoot than others. The relationship of the bore (barrel) to the shooter's wrist can make a gun easy to fire accurately, or can add hours of training to overcome the gun's upward recoil with each shot fired. A gun with a low bore axis (a barrel that sits nearly in line with the wrist and arm) is easier to shoot and takes advantage of the human ability to raise the arm and accurately point the index finger at the center of an object.

The best handguns are designed to place the barrel in close alignment to the wrist and arm, transferring the recoil directly into the shooter's palm and web of the hand, fleshy areas that can absorb the impact painlessly. Because the low barrel aligns with skeletal support of the wrist and arm, the muzzle rises less during shooting, and the shooter can get the sights back on target for rapid consecutive shots—an important consideration in self defense against multiple assailants or

Heckler & Koch's P7M8 has a very low bore axis, making it easy to aim and shoot. It also fits small hands extremely well.

single assailants who are not stopped by the first bullet. Examples of low bore axis semi-automatics include Glock and the Heckler & Koch P7 line of handguns. The Smith and Wesson Centennial revolver has an unusually high backstrap that results in a de facto low bore axis, and an extremely pointable .38 caliber revolver.

If I can only have one, which should I choose?

Most first-time gun owners buy their weapon thinking it will be the only handgun they'll ever own. Later, many find they need to refine their selection after experience introduces them to better fitting or functioning guns; others graduate from a gun purchased for in-house defense to a smaller gun that they can carry with them everywhere. If, at the outset, the buyer is looking for an all-around gun, compact handguns will be the natural choice.

A number of .38 revolvers fit that description. Good choices include the Smith & Wesson Centennial line, which features a completely shrouded hammer, or the bobbed hammer Taurus model 85CH, one of the finest budget priced revolvers available. Both are good choices for concealment beneath clothing that could catch on the hammer when the gun is drawn.

Revolvers with exposed hammers can be entrusted to a gunsmith to bob the hammer, with results similar to the Taurus M85CH. I once considered the Ruger SP101 for such an operation. Because the .357 magnum is chambered in the same SP101 frame as the .38, I would purchase the heavy-hitting .357, but practice with lighter .38 ammunition. Since the .357 case is only slightly longer than the .38's, a .357 revolver can fire .38 ammunition for reduced recoil or for economical practice. (A .38 cannot fire .357 ammunition.) Ruger must have read my mind, because they now manufacture a bobbed hammer version of this gun!

Budget revolvers are generally a safer choice than budget semi-automatics, because of the simpler design of the revolver. In 1992, a perfectly fine .38 revolver from Rossi was marketed for around $200—considerably less than the $400 price on the smoother and more widely-recognized Smith & Wessons and Rugers. Used revolvers should be even cheaper. Novice buyers can check for wear, like a bulged barrel or excessive wiggle when the cylinder is locked, and visually check for cracks and wear on the frame and top strap. There's simply less to go wrong on a used revolver than on a second-hand semi-automatic.

Revolver selection requires the buyer to think about concealability, frame size, and fit in the hand, and probably about after-market replacement grips. The small five-shot revolvers fit small hands better and are more comfortable to conceal. Holstered inside the pants, the revolver's round cylinder can be uncomfortable. Six shot revolvers, by virtue of room for that extra bullet, poke a larger cylinder into the wearer's tummy or hip.

A revolver's fit can be adjusted by replacing the factory-installed grips with after-market grips designed to change the distance between backstrap and trigger, to increase or decrease the circumference of the grips, and to fill in the void between the back of the trigger guard and the grips. Large rubbery grips add more material to absorb the recoil and are easier to grasp.

Semi-automatic features give the buyer considerable choices in capacity, trigger action, size and location of safeties, slide locks and magazine releases, but fewer choices of how the gun fits in your hand. Some semi-automatic grips are integral to the frame and cannot be changed, so the original fit of the weapon is crucial. The polymer frame Glock pistol is

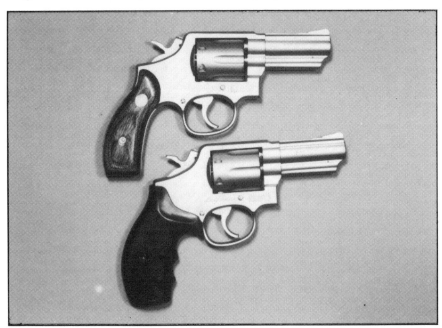

Smith & Wesson revolvers with factory grips (top) and Pachmayr replacement grips.

an example of a gun that needs to fit right the first time, since the grip is the same molded polymer making up the frame. Rubbery sleeves have been offered as after-market grip add-ons for Glocks, but do nothing to reduce the circumference or general shape.

Small or weak-handed people will find certain semi-automatic models easier to shoot effectively. Massad Ayoob suggested several compact semi-autos that are easy to carry, conceal and shoot, including Smith & Wesson's 3913 or 3953, a 9mm with 8-round capacity magazines; and Heckler & Koch's P7M8, a unique 9mm with 8+1 round capacity.

Women often appreciate the short trigger reach of the high-capacity Glock handguns. Caliber choices include 9mm, .40 and .45 caliber, with high capacity magazines holding a whopping nineteen rounds in 9mm to thirteen 45s packed into the Glock 21's magazine. Glock offers their Model 17 and 23, billed as compact versions of the Model 22 and 19. High capacity semi-automatics like the Glocks use a "double-stack" magazine. Instead of stacking the bullets one atop another, as in a single-stack low capacity magazine, the bullets are staggered zig-zag. A double-stack magazine results in a slightly wider grip that will effect the gun's fit in your hand and make the gun a little harder to conceal under clothing.

Glock Model 23 with its double stack magazine.

Compared to high-capacity semi-autos, the HK P7M8 and S & W 3913 are extremely flat and easy to tuck in the waistband. There is less ammunition in the gun, but eight well-placed 9mm bullets should suffice—higher capacity can be an invitation to sloppy shot placement that endangers innocent bystanders. Remember, even under the extreme duress of an assault you are responsible for every bullet you fire.

Right between the 9mm and the big-bore .45 caliber is the relatively new .40 caliber. Developed by Smith & Wesson, this size ammunition is often referred to as .40 S&W, to give credit to the developer. Ballistically, the .40 is expected to show a stopping power at least as good as the 9mm, and it is estimated that +P .40 ammunition should approach the optimum results of the .357 magnum. Examples of .40 caliber handguns include the Glock 22 and 23, Smith & Wesson 4013 and 411, Ruger P91 and others including the Witness and Firestar.

When my female students shoot guns provided for demonstration, they are excited to discover they can shoot the .45s accurately. With the development of high performance .45 hollowpoint ammunition, the venerable .45 has become an excellent self defense handgun. Reacting to the call for lighter, faster bullets, Cor-Bon sells a 185-grain +P .45

The .357 magnum is a manageable gun for the well-trained woman.

caliber bullet that leaves the barrel at 1150 feet per second. And there are .45s available that are small enough for effective concealment.

Good choices for concealable .45s include Firestar's small model .45 with its 6-shot magazine, Colt's Lightweight Commander or Officer's Model and Springfield's Compact .45. A full-sized .45 will be a better choice for competitive shooting, training or to serve solely as a home-defense gun.

How it shoots

An individual's ability to shoot well with a particular handgun is affected by upper body strength and hand size in relation to the dimensions of the gun. Buying a gun recommended by a large number of men may give you a man-sized gun, but one you can't shoot effectively. A fit of machismo at the gun counter is dangerous!

While the gun's fit in your hand can be determined in the sterile atmosphere of a gun store, your reaction to the gun's recoil can be judged only during shooting. Fortunately, good training can help shooters of any size learn to handle even heavy-hitting calibers accurately, although there is a cut-off point after which the time between shots remains pretty much the same, because of the amount of time needed to re-acquire the sight picture on the recoiling gun.

Most indoor gun ranges rent a wide variety of the popular model handguns. This is an excellent way for new shooters to gauge the recoil of .38 caliber, 9mm, .40 and .45 caliber guns and ammunition, before investing several hundred dollars. After choosing an appropriate self defense caliber, the most important decision is the shooter's willingness to train and practice with the handgun. A gun that causes a lot of discomfort during shooting is a gun that will not be shot very much. Weapon unfamiliarity, especially with a single action semi-auto, is a recipe for disaster in self defense situations.

Reliability

So many different factors affect handgun reliability that it is like discussing an individual's reactions to different flavors or scents. Nonetheless, before one adopts a handgun for self defense, the reliability of that weapon must be ascertained. Beginning shooters can consider revolvers more reliable than semi-automatics, in the sense that less can malfunction on a revolver.

Those who favor the semi-automatic owe it to themselves to make a more intensive study of the handgun they are considering buying. Look for reviews in gun magazines, especially seeking out information on reliability, gun malfunctions, and brands of ammunition tested in the weapon. A semi-automatic's reliability, while first a question of design and production standards, is also greatly affected by cleaning and maintenance, and by the specific model's ability to feed specific kinds of ammunition. A self defense weapon *must* cycle high performance hollowpoint ammunition 100% of the time.

After purchasing a handgun, the buyer must test that weapon with the ammunition they plan to carry in it. Revolver shooters should test and occasionally practice with their defense ammunition to remain accustomed to its recoil and to be sure the firing pin strikes the primers with sufficient impact to fire the round. Semi-automatic owners need to run a minimum of 150-200 rounds of their defense ammunition through their handgun to guarantee flawless feeding of the ammunition into

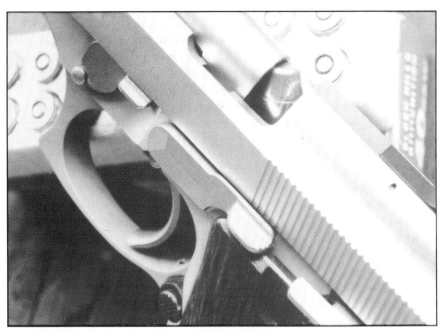

A semi-automatic handgun must fire, eject and chamber the ammunition you intend to carry for self defense 100% of the time. A feed failure is shown here. The bullet should have traveled horizontally into the chamber, but has risen vertically and now protrudes out of the ejection port, jamming the handgun.

the chamber and reliable ejection of the empty case after the round is fired. If the testing produces several malfunctions, repeat the process with a different ammunition, until you have found hollowpoint ammunition that always functions in your self defense gun. If nothing cycles reliably in the gun, you may need to visit the gunsmith for a bit of fine-tuning.

Many serviceable handguns are marketed. The buyer's responsibility is to select one with which they can safely train and practice. The gun needs to be concealable (if the owner intends to carry it outside the home) and must have adequate safety features to assure it will not be unintentionally discharged. Very low budget semi-autos are infamous for lacking firing pin blocks that keep the hammer from striking the firing pin unless the trigger is pulled all the way through its cycle. These guns may fire if dropped or jarred—the impact bounces the firing pin forward to strike the ammunition, and a bullet is fired in very unsafe circumstances. Read up on the gun you intend to purchase, and ask the gun store clerk about the internal safeties of the model you are considering. If this is the only kind of gun you can afford, either buy a less expensive used revolver or carry the thing with a full magazine, but *never* leave a round in the chamber where an accidental impact might cause the gun to fire.

These are serious questions. One of the easiest ways to find the answers is to postpone a handgun purchase until *after* you have completed at least one basic handgun training course. Your basic training should have put you in touch with qualified professionals who can answer any questions that remain after the course curriculum has been completed. Study first, buy later.

Getting to know your gun

Cleaning your weapon is an excellent way to understand how it works. A gun isn't like a car that you can turn over to a mechanic every 3,000 miles for an oil change and safety check. A gun is an emergency rescue tool. If it malfunctions, you must understand how to correct the problem immediately and get back in the gun fight. A thorough understanding of its functions is crucial.

Initially, you'll need to ask the clerk selling you the gun to take a few uninterrupted minutes to show you how to take the gun apart and clean it. You have just plunked several hundred dollars down on the counter. Don't be shy about asking for this small service before you walk out the door with your new gun. The owner's manuals usually have a section on cleaning the weapon, although some do not. Another source of gun cleaning information is a small book titled *The Professional's Guide to Gun Cleaning*, by Marty Hayes.[1] Complete with pictures and written instruction, this guide should get you through a safe and efficient gun cleaning.

When I bought my first gun, the clerk assembled a list of cleaning supplies, which I purchased on his recommendation. I went home and for the next month or so cleaned my revolver without realizing the cylinder could be removed for a more convenient and thorough cleaning. My first basic shooting class included a section on gun cleaning, and I was thrilled to learn the easy, correct way to clean that gun. Find a teacher who will work with your gun cleaning questions and demonstrate that skill in the course curriculum.

---

[1] Hayes, Marty, *The Professional's Guide to Gun Cleaning*, FAS Books, P.O. Box 2814, Kirkland, WA 98083.

14
Shotguns, Rifles and Carbines

While the handgun is more versatile and portable, the ensconced defender can put a rifle or shotgun to very effective use defending herself and her family. Though their use is more situation-dependent, under certain circumstances, shotguns fill a role in the self defense armory that can be filled by no other firearm.

During the 1992 riots in Los Angeles, the weapon found most valuable for intimidation was the shotgun, reports law enforcement trainer John Farnam. Report after report surfaced where the defender raised the shotgun to their shoulder, to find the aggressors had suddenly decided to loot and destroy a different structure. By now you know I'm diametrically opposed to people considering their weapons for intimidation alone. However, Farnam relates incidents from his police work in which an offender ignored *or completely failed to see and acknowledge* his drawn handgun. Farnam concludes that no one mistakes the deadly intent of a shotgun being raised to the shoulder.

Shotgun

The shotgun is a practical, effective home defense weapon. The large shells contain from nine to twenty shot balls that can be fired in one lethal burst. The shotgun is best employed in a controlled fire zone, with all innocents safely *behind* the muzzle. Any shotgun load lethal enough to stop an oncoming assailant is also heavy enough to penetrate walls and harm anyone behind it.

If you have chosen a shotgun that fits your height and build, you may find the long gun easier to shoot accurately under stress than a handgun. Held at arm's length, a handgun trembles with a shaking hand. A shotgun can be pressed firmly into the pectoral muscle, supported with both arms and held steadier than the smaller handgun.

The shotgun's longer sight radius thrusts the front sight into the cone of vision that remains during the effects of tunnel vision. Held in the high ready position, the shotgun's muzzle is visible in the area the defender is scanning for approaching danger.

About the only bad point, beyond problems caused by an ill-fitting shotgun or one that creates too powerful a blast for a smaller person to control, is the necessity to use both hands to effectively fire the shotgun. An injury, or use of a hand to hold a child out of harm's way, will make using a shotgun very difficult. Therefore, its best deployment is in an ensconced defender's scenario, where the adult has gathered or safely sequestered the children, and is waiting in the safe room or at the head of the hallway to defend the family if the assailant disregards commands to advance no farther.

The defender needs to be able to fire consecutive blasts with the shotgun. A person under the influence of drugs, rage or fight-flight reaction takes longer to react, and can continue to fight after your first volley hits. No weapon, not even the potent 12 gauge shotgun, can guarantee an instant stop. Train yourself to make follow-up shots; they may well be necessary. If a lethal assault justified the use of deadly force in your defense, the second blast is equally justified, unless the assailant has fallen or turned to run.

Two members of the three-woman-team of (L to R) Lyn Bates, Connie Gabielska, and Deb Higgins fire 12 gauge shotguns at the one-of-a-kind Second Chance Bowling pin shoot.

Autoloaders or pump

Self defense shoppers have two basic styles of shotguns to consider: (a) the semi-auto and (b) the pump or slide action shotgun.

Like semi-automatic handguns, the semi-automatic shotgun captures gases from the burning gunpowder or uses the recoil of the shot to eject the empty case and chamber a fresh cartridge for the next shot. By doing most of the work for you, the semi-auto leaves the shooter free to fully concentrate on the sights and on a smooth, controlled trigger press.

Semi-automatic shotguns will cost more than pump guns, but are preferable for defense because of low recoil and fast shot-to-shot time.

Probably the nicest semi-automatic shotgun is the Benelli Super 90. Unfortunately, this 12 gauge shotgun has a hefty recoil, although it is favored for its ruggedness and reliability. In 20 gauge semi-autos, Massad Ayoob recommends the Remington 1100 or the 11-87.

Pump shotguns have a sliding fore end that the shooter pulls back to eject the empty shell and feed a fresh round from the magazine onto the shell lift. The forward stroke feeds the shell into the chamber. Sound complicated? It is, and the backward and forward strokes cannot be incomplete or a malfunction will result. The slide-action shotgun requires experience and physical coordination, and usually gives slower shot-to-shot times. Its cost, on the other hand, is about half that of semi-autos.

Pump or slide-action shotgun choices include the Mossberg 500 or 590. I like the Mossberg design because the thumb safety is on the top of the tang. It seems the most natural place for the thumb to rest and operate this vital button. Another respectable choice would be Remington's 870, favored by many police agencies that use the pump shotgun.

Twelve gauge or twenty gauge

Just like handguns, shotguns are sized to accommodate different strengths and body sizes. In self defense shotgun discussions, the 12 gauge often dominates, simply because it has been the shotgun chosen by police for decades. Since it is respected in police circles, it is often the choice of civilians and the recommendation of gun store clerks. 12 gauge, 20 gauge or the less-common 16-gauge is determined by a formula stating that 12 round balls the diameter of the 12-gauge shotgun's barrel weigh a pound. It takes twenty balls the diameter of the smaller 20 gauge shotgun's barrel to weigh a pound, so the 20 gauge fires a smaller cartridge.

The 12 gauge, because of its larger barrel, can expel greater quantities of shot or a larger slug than the 20 gauge. The powder charge required to fire the larger load, however, will recoil into the shooter with almost double the force of a 20 gauge. While the average female shooter may be large enough to take the impact of the recoil, the time required to make a follow-up shot will be longer, and seconds count for everything during a self defense shooting.

For practical reasons, I favor the smaller 20 gauge shotgun. An even smaller shotgun was marketed to women a few years back, the .410 shotgun from Mossberg. It is too small for self defense: hunters find it ineffective against deer, so don't trust your life to this under-powered, undersized firearm.

Shotgun ammunition

One of the drawbacks of using a handgun for self defense is the puny stopping power of one bullet. Every defensive shooting instructor I've encountered trains students to fire multiple shots, since a single round

Cutaway of shotgun shells: (L-R) 12 gauge slug, 12 gauge shell with 00 buckshot, 20 gauge cartridge with the smaller #3 buckshot.

Self-defense with the shotgun requires an aggressively forward posture to control the recoil of consecutive shots.

is unlikely to bring an instant cessation to hostile activity. The shotgun lets you fire multiple shot balls in a single blast.

Ammunition choices for the shotgun range from the tiny (not-recommended) birdshot and small game shot, to the more deadly buckshot, up to the shotgun slug. Buckshot is packaged in different sizes, indicating choices of different quantities and sizes of shot balls. Buckshot is an excellent ammunition choice, since a blast of nine to twenty balls of shot, depending on the shell chosen, wounds multiple organs, nerves, vessels, and bones, as well as creating a "rat hole" wound in soft tissue when fired from close range.

Buckshot is effective at distances up to 15 yards. Beyond 15 yards, the pattern spread is generally too wide to be effective. Few bedrooms are more than 15 yards across, making the 20 gauge shotgun loaded with #3 buckshot an exceedingly good defense selection.

In the very shootable 20 gauge shotgun, #3 buckshot fits twenty .25 caliber pellets into a manageable load with devastating hit potential. Twenty-gauge shooters could also load with the hard-hitting slug, a projectile weighing 5/8 of an ounce. For the hale and hearty, 12 gauge shotgun shells are available in 000 buckshot, eight .36 caliber balls; 00 buckshot, nine .33 caliber balls; #1 buckshot with sixteen .30 caliber balls. A 12 gauge slug typically weighs one ounce and measures .72 caliber in diameter.

Birdshot or small game shot in either 20 or 12 gauge is not recommended. It is sometimes suggested for urban use, on the premise that it will not penetrate sheet rock walls and harm innocent people behind the walls. Wrong—sheet rock is easy to penetrate (ever see a brother or boyfriend put his fist through a wall in a fit of temper?) Birdshot *will* penetrate sheet rock walls and can harm family members, but cannot be trusted to stop a determined assailant. Jan Libourel, writing in Peterson's Handguns in November of 1990, reminded readers that even at the relatively close distances entailed in a home defense situation, "small shot may disperse so much that it will be unlikely to strike a disabling blow, especially against a heavily-clad adversary."

In addition to using good quality ammunition, a shotgun needs to be kept clean and well-maintained. Gas-operated shotguns are especially unforgiving when fouled by residue left behind from practice shooting.

Best shooting techniques

Fixing the sights on the target is easier with a shotgun than a handgun, because the length of the weapon gives more for the eye to compare and align. Basic shooting principles apply: focus on the front sight as it centers on the target. A smooth trigger squeeze with the sights aligned will give perfect shot placement. Trigger weights on most shotguns are light, requiring only three to five pounds of pressure to fire the gun.

Fast, consecutive shots with the shotgun require what may seem at first an extreme body position to keep the shooter balanced. The forward leg should be sharply bent, with the muscles taut. The rear leg, straight or nearly straight, is well back, and the distance between the feet is shoulder width or a little more.

Because the shotgun has a powerful recoil, the shoulders need to be well forward of the hips, and the hips forward of the knee, which is forward of the foot of the rear leg. The entire body is leaning aggressively into the butt plate of the shotgun. The head tucks down, to position the cheekbone against the comb of the stock, bringing the eyes down to a level at which they can view the front sight when it is aligned with the rear.

The non-dominant hand supports the long, heavy shotgun at the fore end. On semi-automatic guns, it is purely supportive. On a pump shotgun, the non-dominant hand cycles the slide between shots. The stock of the shotgun, crafted from wood, plastic, or laminate, can be cut down to give the shooter the proper length from the base of the shotgun to the fore end. A shotgun that is too long forces the shooter's shoulders too far back and keeps her off balance as consecutive blasts from the shotgun push her body backward.

The dominant hand's fingers are wrapped behind the trigger guard, with the trigger finger resting outside the trigger guard when the firearm is not sighted on the target, ready to fire. The thumb of the dominant hand rests atop the gun, riding the safety on Mossbergs and similar shotguns.

Even if the safety is located behind the trigger, as many are, the thumb must ride atop the shotgun. It is a natural impulse to wrap the thumb all the way around the shotgun, trying to enclose it in a strong fist to increase control. Don't do it! The knuckles of a wrapped-around thumb will jump back during recoil and knock your glasses askew or strike your tender nose, causing bleeding, watery eyes, and other natural pain responses.

The greatest discomfort traditionally associated with shooting a shotgun comes from allowing the recoiling stock to strike painfully into the bony shoulder joint. Lock the stock in tightly, in past the shoulder joint, below the clavicle. When the firing arm's elbow extends out shoulder high or higher, the pectoral muscle rises up and cushions this part of your chest, so shooting the gun doesn't hurt!

Some people, even after learning the shooting position described above, are discomfited by the impact of the comb against the cheek, and by the recoil transferred to the body. Should they simply give up the shotgun? No! There is a solution for shooters who really don't want discomfort.

Since the shotgun has a long barrel and sight radius, the front sight can be visible and centered on the target for effective close-range defensive shooting at seven yards or less, without having the shotgun mounted at the shoulder. The "High Tuck" position, a completely pain-free shooting technique is described fully in Massad Ayoob's *Stressfire II,*[1] and is reason enough alone to purchase and study the book.

Author fires the 12 gauge Remington 1100 in the High-Tuck position discussed in this chapter.

The High Tuck position's accuracy depends on tucking the stock of the shotgun tightly into the armpit. The comb touches the tendons in the arm pit. The dominant arm locks down on the stock and the hand takes a firm grip at the tang. Keep the middle finger well away from the trigger guard, if you can. Don't get sloppy with the hand's grip—while learning this position, I have given myself deep bruises on the middle knuckle by relaxing into a loose grip while shooting in the high tuck position. The shotgun's recoil will push the shotgun rearward since the buttstock recoils beyond the shooter's body and arm. The tighter the arm locks down, the less recoil movement the shooter will have to overcome.

Since the shotgun has a substantial recoil, shooters will find it easier to fire repeated shots from a standing position. If your protective cover forces you into a crouch, kneel with one knee up, the other knee wide out and far to the rear, with the foot of the rear leg trailing far, far behind the body. The head and shoulders are aggressively forward. The trailing leg gives the shooter a large supporting base to keep the body from being driven backward by the recoil.

Tactics

The shotgun is an excellent survival tool for the defender ensconced in a safe room, ready to defend self and family if the intruder ignores warnings and comes through the door. This scenario presumes that the defender knows the zones of fire, knows the direction in which the shotgun pellets will travel, and knows beyond any doubt that no innocents are in the path of the shotgun blast. It is best applied to home layouts where children's rooms lie behind the defender. In home layouts where rooms are scattered about, young children will need to be quietly taken to the safe area before firing begins.

In apartments, safe rooms *must* be arranged so the fire zone is backed by bullet stopping material—something in short supply in urban housing. While nothing short of heavy concrete construction gives full bullet stopping ability, careful shot placement into *known* uninhabited directions is necessary for those who plan to use the shotgun's multiple pellets in home defense.

The shotgun is not the best weapon to take prowling through your house to check out a noise in the night. Not only are house searches dangerous, the long muzzle of the shotgun gives an intruder lurking behind a doorway advance warning of your approach, and offers a lever to grab. The shotgun's size makes it more difficult to move quietly, avoiding furniture, lamps and other household objects. Return to lesson one: don't indulge in house searches if you really believe you have an intruder in the home!

Weapon retention techniques have been developed for the shotgun; if you adopt this weapon you owe it to yourself and your loved ones to get the proper training in its use and retention. Know how to accurately shoot your shotgun, and know how to keep it in your hands if the assailant survives the blast and tries to take it from you.

Rifles and carbines: long range power

Evan Marshall believes the rifle fills several roles in civilian self defense. Many people simply find the "long gun" easier to accept. They've been socialized to accept rifles and shotguns as legitimate, having seen them in the hands of their fathers and grandfathers as hunting tools. Some people are simply unwilling to learn to shoot the shotgun. They've been told the recoil will be painful, and they may be unable to find suitable training. The rifle may appeal to this person.

Some jurisdictions deny citizens the right to own a handgun. Because of the social acceptance for hunting sports, ownership of a rifle or pistol-caliber carbine may be acceptable.

Is there any place for the rifle in the civilian self defense arsenal? I asked John and Vicki Farnam, who responded with a story.

A woman and her children were in their remote Montana home when a warning came over the radio that authorities believed an escaped, dangerous prisoner was in their area. The announcement put the woman in a heightened state of awareness, and somewhat later she spotted a lone figure walking up her mile-and-a-half driveway.

Standing on her porch, rifle in hand, she ordered the man to come no closer. The stranger ignored repeated verbal warnings, and when he kept coming, the woman shot him in one knee. Displaying determined aggression, the man kept coming. Her second shot took out his other knee. The woman held him for the law enforcement officers, who confirmed her fear that she had indeed encountered the escapee.

The value of the rifle in personal defense, John Farnam concluded, is its ability to deliver highly accurate hits at distances that are beyond the accuracy range of the handgun. "We're hearing the term 'urban rifle' to describe a rifle used for defense between 30 and 150 meters," Farnam explained. These distances allow target identification and verbal warnings, both vital elements of legally justifiable self defense shootings.

Farnam recommends the .223 (5.56 in metric terms) caliber rifle as one of the most practical for civilian use. This caliber has an effective range of up to 200 meters. Greater distances are the speciality of snipers, and at even 200 meters, the possibility for retreat and escape is likely a better option. "Almost any normal person is capable of good, consistent hits at 100 to 200 meters in 99.99% of most military rifle situations," Farnam continued. He defines military rifle skill as a hit on any part of the body, since an army's goal is to take the fighting man off the field.

In civilian self defense, the goal must be the immediate cessation of hostile activity. To accomplish that, Farnam recommends a shot to the head. Traveling 3000 feet per second, there is no danger of the bullet skidding around the cranium, as there is with a handgun bullet. The ballistics of the rifle cartridge gives us a small bullet moving at extreme velocities. A common .223 caliber rifle bullet, for instance, weighs just 55 grains and travels at 3200 feet per second. The .223 is a popular choice of shooters who favor the Colt AR-15. The Ruger Mini-

Shooting the Colt AR-15, using simulated cover for training.

14 is also chambered for the .223 round, and is one of the top choices for a small rifle for civilian defense.

Massad Ayoob recommends Ruger's Mini-14 for small-statured people, and specifically women, as discussed in the July 1993 edition of *Shooting Industry*. For larger rifles, Ayoob suggests a telescoping after market stock replacement for AR-15 style rifles. This stock closes down to fit small people, but can be extended to fit a larger spouse, he suggests.

High velocity rifles are risky in urban situations. The tiny bullet traveling at incredible speed will go through wall after wall, posing danger to people nearby. Choose the rifle for low-density situations where the identified target may be beyond the range of your handgun.

An alternative to the "urban" rifle is a long gun chambered for a pistol cartridge, Farnam pointed out. "Some people argue that a carbine is just a big, clumsy handgun," Farnam grinned, "but that's not true." He noted that this kind of carbine has a considerably longer sight radius than a pistol, that handgun bullets develop much higher velocities in the long barrel and these guns generally have sights far superior to the handgun.

Marlin Camp Carbine, chambered for 9mm ammunition. The scope has been added to this gun for hunting small game.

The pistol cartridge-chambered carbine recoils considerably less than a handgun and is relatively quiet when fired. These features make them very pleasant firearms with which to practice. Farnam reported that he has seen women shoot hundreds of rounds in comfort, becoming deadly accurate in the process. These carbines are excellent "companion" guns to the handgun, because the owner can purchase one caliber of ammunition for use in both weapons.

The carbine offers good accuracy to 100 meters, for threat management where an assailant has been clearly identified and has ignored warnings to leave. One of the best-known choices for this kind of firearm is the Marlin Camp Carbine. Most civilians won't shoot enough rounds to wear the Marlin out, although Evan Marshall, of Detroit police fame, reported that some police departments had attempted to put the Marlin Camp Carbine into use and found it would not stand up to the rigors of law enforcement training and day-to-day use. Farnam recommended the HK 94 as an alternate, although you will pay much more for this weapon than the popular little Marlin.

15

Ammunition

Handgun ammunition comes in so many varieties that the beginning shooter often feels overwhelmed by the task of selecting ammunition for self defense. Often it falls to a clerk in the gun store to recommend ammunition to the first-time gun buyer. These folks are sincere in their desire to help, but I'd rather not rely on a stranger to select a vital component in my self defense provisions.

The crew at one Seattle-area gun range is probably still snickering about the woman who asked for a box of Federal Hydra-Shoks by requesting the "cartridge that causes a great hydrostatic shock if it is fired into a body." The clerk grinned and replied, "Lady, that describes most of the ammunition behind this counter." Well, quit snickering, guys, because that woman was me. When I started shooting, I bought a box of 20 Hydra-Shok hollowpoints for my 2-inch snub nosed revolver on the advice of the gun store clerk. I would now prefer to have been matched up with a higher velocity load, but as earlier noted, the clerks do sincerely try to match the new shooter with a reliable ammunition for their new gun.

Ammunition selection is a task complicated by the new shooter's ignorance of terms and vocabulary to communicate their needs, concerns and desires. Let us, then, hold a little vocabulary session.

Ammunition terminology

Round or Cartridge: One unit of ammunition, comprised of a bullet, a case, a primer and gunpowder. You will also hear the word "load" used informally to describe a round of ammunition or a variety of ammunition.

Caliber: The diameter of the bullet at its base, measured in 100ths or 1000ths of an inch. Thus, a .45 caliber bullet is 45/100ths of an inch in diameter, a .357 caliber bullet is 357/1000ths of an inch in diameter. Bullet diameter is also measured in millimeters. The European-born 9mm ammunition is a good example of bullet diameter measured in millimeters.

Bullet: The projectile that is seated in the top of the case, and is fired out of the gun.

Bullet Weight: Bullets are identified, first by caliber (diameter), then by weight. Bullet weight is defined in a unit called grains: 7000 grains equal one pound. It is common to hear discussion of a 9mm 115-grain hollowpoint bullet, referring to a bullet weighing 115 grains that measures 9mm in diameter at the base.

Hollowpoint, Roundnose and Ball: Bullets come in a multitude of shapes for various uses. The most common are hollowpoint, roundnose and ball, either lead or jacketed, and the lead semi-wadcutters and full wadcutters.

Wadcutter

Wadcutter: A bullet that is a cylinder of lead, some with flat ends on both top and bottom, others with a cavity hollowed out at the base. The bullet is seated flush with the top of the case, and is used primarily for revolver target shooting.

Semi-wadcutter

Semi-wadcutter: A bullet that somewhat resembles the wadcutter (hence its name) but tapers to a smaller, flat top. It is used in both revolvers and semi-automatic handguns as target and practice ammunition.

Roundnose: Also a practice ammunition valued for its reliable feeding in semi-automatic handguns. It consists of a round-nosed bullet, either jacketed or lead, and is less expensive than hollowpoint bullets.

Roundnose lead

Hollowpoint

Hollowpoint: Hollowpoints resemble a roundnose bullet with a deep hole cut into top of the bullet. The hollowed out section causes the lead bullet to expand to a mushroom-like shape when it encounters tissue. The expansion increases the size of the projectile, causing a larger wound channel and more tissue disruption for quicker cessation of hostilities. This is the only bullet you should carry for self defense. Not only does it stop hostilities sooner, it generally stops inside the body of the assailant, dramatically reducing the danger that your bullet will go all the way through the assailant's body and hit an innocent bystander.

FMJ: Full metal jacketed ammunition consists of a lead projectile fully encased in a copper jacket. This ammunition is free of the lubricant found on lead ammunition since the copper jacket slips easily through the gun's barrel when fired. Since there is no lubricant, it produces considerably less smoke when fired, and because the lead bullet is enclosed in the jacket, reduces lead exposure.

Case: The metal cylinder and base that holds the gunpowder, bullet and primer. Generally made of brass, but also seen in stainless steel and one-use disposable aluminum. While the strength of the case is important, it is the firearm's chamber that supports the case walls and keeps the case from blowing apart while the burning powder is building up pressure to push the bullet out of the top of the case.

Primer: A small ignition "cap" seated in an indentation in the base of the case which, when hit by the handgun's firing pin, ignites and transfers a spark to ignite the gunpowder inside the case. The primer's function could be compared to that of an automobile spark plug.

Powder: Gunpowder, when ignited by the primer, burns rapidly, building up pressure inside the case until it forces the bullet from the top of the case a through the barrel of the gun. The proportion of powder to airspace in the case affects the pressures that build up while the powder burns, and the velocity with which that pressure pushes the bullet through the gun barrel and out the muzzle.

ACP, S&W, Luger and Parabellum: Caliber designations that gives credit to the inventor of the particular caliber ammunition in question. Example: .380 or .45 Auto Colt Pistol; .40 Smith & Wesson, and 9mm Luger or 9mm Parabellum. 9mm Luger and 9mm Parabellum are exactly the same size, and both can be fired through any 9mm handgun. However, 9mm Kurz, 9mm Corto, and 9mm Short are terms used to describe .380 ammunition, which *is* different than 9mm Parabellum or 9mm Luger.

Velocity: The speed at which the bullet travels is measured in feet per second. Thus, on boxes of "high performance" ammunition, you may find a declaration of how fast the bullet will travel. For instance on a high velocity 9mm, the bullet weight may be stated, followed by the words 1350 fps, indicating that when shot from an average length gun barrel, the bullet traveled at 1350 feet per second when it left the muzzle.

Velocity is determined by how much pressure builds up in the case as the gunpowder burns, the weight of the bullet, and of the length of the barrel of the handgun. Smaller, lighter bullets travel faster, and according to current opinion, cause greater shock and tissue disruption in the target, bringing a faster cessation to the hostilities.

+P or +P+, Subsonic and Magnum: Subsonic ammunition expels the bullet at speeds under 1000 feet per second. +P indicates ammunition designed to generate higher pressures than standard ammunition and +P+ is a very high pressure load. Magnum ammunition, best known as the .357 and .44 magnum calibers, have additional powder to build enormous pressures before the bullet is expelled. Thus, a .357 magnum cartridge may have a bullet velocity from 1350 to 1450 feet per second.

Stopping Power and One-Shot Stops: Since humans began the study of ballistics, theories about what made ammunition effective have proliferated. Included in these theories are the Relative Incapacitation Index, the FBI Multimedia Wound Value, and many others. They make great reading for insomniacs, but frankly, unless you are a data cruncher, these theories are harder than heck to assimilate. Furthermore, the theories are just that: theories. That is why I am an enthusiastic student of Evan Marshall and his study of one-shot stops, which we shall discuss forthwith.

Evan, Ed, and the one-shot stops

Evan Marshall, a twenty-year veteran of the Detroit Police Department, spent over 15 years collecting data from actual "street" shootings. Evan and Ed Sanow, an engineer and law enforcement officer, co-authored *Handgun Stopping Power, The Definitive Study*. This best-selling gun book draws on Evan's studies of police reports about the shootings, evidence technicians' records, statements from surviving victims, autopsy files and photos. Ed is a law enforcement professional and a regular contributor to the top gun magazines, writing about different ammunitions and educating readers about ballistics.

This informative volume is easy to read, containing actual stories about shootings to illustrate the ability of different cartridges to stop an assailant. The best, a one-shot stop, occurs when one round of ammunition stops continued activity by the individual taking the bullet. Don't let the term lull you into believing that one bullet—even one with optimum ballistics—will always stop an assailant. Placement of that shot in a vulnerable part of the anatomy is usually the reason the assailant stopped after being hit only once. There are, however, some kinds of ammunition that are more destructive than others. *Handgun Stopping Power* relates the successes and failures of various calibers, bullet weights and brands of ammunition.

It would be difficult to summarize the data and reports Marshall and Sanow gathered for *Handgun Stopping Power*. This is a book you should borrow or buy and read.[1] Your decision about ammunition for your own protection can be based on information from actual shootings. Until you can get your copy of this book, remember the following:

Your self defense ammunition should be hollowpoint. It should have a muzzle velocity of 1000 fps or greater for reliable hollowpoint expansion and maximum energy transfer when it hits the target. Faster velocities are desirable. Go to the range and experiment with several brands and velocities of ammunition until you find one you can fire in accurate rapid-fire simulation of a self defense emergency. The fastest velocities, like the largest calibers, may produce more recoil than you can control effectively if you are of small, light build. Good choices, in a nutshell, will begin with the .38 Special +P; for some the .357 magnum will be manageable; the 9mm in +P or +P+ may well be the best overall choice; +P .40 caliber is a popular alternative between 9mm and .45 caliber.

Women should not rule out carrying a .45 if they have received good training and practice regularly with that caliber of handgun and ammunition. I recently took top score in a week-long firearms instructor training course put on by the Washington State Criminal Justice Commission. I shot a .45 caliber Springfield 1911 A1. Firearms Academy of Seattle associate instructor, DeAnne Orive, took second place shooting a .45 caliber Para-Ordnance. We were the only women in an eleven person class, and used the opportunity to prove that women can shoot accurately, even with large handguns.

I would caution you to be really sure you can handle the recoil of the .357 magnum, .44 magnum, and 10mm before carrying it for self defense. The magnums and 10mm recoil viciously and will slow your shot-to-shot times. A good test of your ability to use a handgun in self defense is the 5 in 5 at 5 test I use in my gun test articles. Run a target out to five yards. Load the gun. Have a friend time you, saying, "go," and at the end of five seconds, yelling, "stop!" If you have fired five rounds inside a 5-inch radius in five seconds at the practical self defense distance of five yards, you have found a gun you can use effectively for self defense.

Most authorities do not recommend ammunition/handgun calibers below .380 ACP. Marshall and Sanow showed the .380 semi-automatic ammunition rendered one-shot stops in 52 to 65 percent of the shootings studied. .38 Specials loaded to +P pressures were one-shot effective 50 to 75 percent of the time, with a lot of performance variation between ammunition brands and bullet weight. In comparison, the 9mm shootings showed between 62 and 89 percent of the ammunitions involved rendered one-shot stops. There are many variables: effective-

Shooting the .45 well can be a rewarding experience.

ness of the ammunition, accuracy of the shot placement and individual qualities of the person shot, including substance abuse, determination or rage.

Finally, there is no magic bullet. Accurate shot placement is of utmost importance. The most viable target is the center of the chest at armpit level. This increases the chances of a heart, lung or spinal cord hit. In addition, a center-of-mass aim point is quickest for the adrenaline-pumped defender. Additional discussion of shot placement is included in Tactics, Chapter 17. Students of armed self defense must learn to shoot *until the threat ceases.* Unless the spinal cord is severed or the brain's medulla oblongata hit, the assailant may be capable of continued hostilities after taking several handgun bullets. You must be capable of repeated, accurate shots to the center of the assailant's chest.

Misses don't count in a gunfight, and in the end, your life is the prize.

[1] Marshall, Evan, and Sanow, Ed, *Handgun Stopping Power: The Definitive Study.* Paladin Press, 1992.

16
Carrying a Gun When You Need It

With so much violent crime occurring on the street, how can a gun left at home protect you when you are outside? Can you predict when you will become a victim of violent crime? A chore as innocuous as a trip to the store can throw you into contact with an assailant. It is unwise to assume that familiar shopping centers are danger free. Can you guarantee—beyond any doubt—that your car will reach your destination trouble free? Or that you won't be involved in an accident on the way? Can you be sure of the character of every person in the parking lot or of the tow truck driver if your car breaks down?

Of course not. Most of us go about our day-to-day duties without using a weapon, but the one-in-three woman who *will* become a victim of violence in her lifetime can't chose the moment the attack will come. *We simply cannot predict when or where we will need to protect ourselves.* I won't play roulette with my daily well-being, so I always carry a gun.

Daily wear and care

The sad truth is that there isn't an utterly comfortable way to wear a concealed handgun. The best we can hope for, first and foremost, is complete concealment of the gun, fine tuning the comfort with various holsters, maybe even with various models of the firearm you wish to carry. Winter clothing will accommodate a larger, generally higher capacity handgun than the lighter garb of summer. Owning two guns, one large, the other small, with comparable locations for safety and magazine releases can make it easier to carry a gun all the time.

Another sad truth is that it often takes several purchases to find the right holster for you and your gun. Nearly every gun owner I know jokes about wanting to have a holster garage sale. Like me, they own several holsters per gun, some they know they will never use again. The following words may keep new gun owners from stockpiling too many holsters for the great garage sale in the sky.

I personally like a holster I can conceal in what is called the appendix carry—tucked in the concave curve between abdomen and strong-side hip. It was recommended for me when I was first carrying a five-shot revolver—I continued to use it when I carried the larger Glock 23, and when climate allowed an over shirt or vest to conceal the gun. Although the gun seems obvious to the wearer in this position, it is not a place where viewers stare. A woman's figure is studied in the buttocks, hip or chest. The belly is not subject to that much scrutiny. The appendix carry is very fast to draw from, and the only downside I've discovered is that it requires a closed vest or shirt to conceal it. In the summer, when my colleagues are wearing tank tops and open front vests, I have to wear an over-shirt big enough to button and conceal the gun. With a small, flat semi-automatic like the Smith & Wesson 3913, I like an inside-the-waistband holster tucked right behind my strong-side hip. This allows me to conceal the gun while wearing a light vest or shirt over a tank top or t-shirt. In this mode of carry, one learns not to lean over in public, since the outline of the gun butt protrudes without the upright torso to mask it. In the grocery store, for instance, I'll squat to pick up items on low shelves instead of just bending over to collect them.

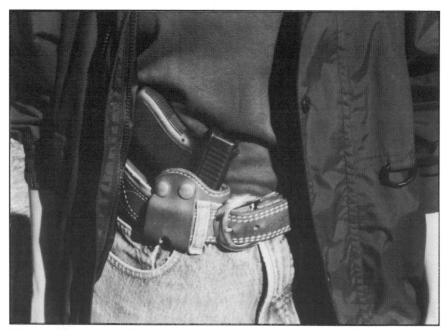

The appendix carry puts a lot of restrictions on the clothing concealing the handgun since it rides ahead of the hip. It is demonstrated here using a Milt Sparks Executive Companion, which can also be carried on or behind the hip comfortably.

Light clothing will generally cover up a snub-nosed five-shot revolver in an inside-the-waistband holster like the Milt Sparks Summer Special shown below or a pancake holster worn just slightly behind the hip.

The primary holster choice for concealed carry of any gun should be a high-quality inside-the-waistband holster. There are numerous variations, but you should insist on a holster with a rigid mouth that remains open after the gun is drawn. Generally, a spring steel band will be enclosed in leather, to keep the holster's "mouth" open for safe, one-handed holstering. Other holsters rely on very stiff construction, like Greg Kramer's premium-quality gun leather, made of very tough horse-hide that stays open without the gun to support the sides.

This is a vital feature: should you find yourself holding an assailant at gun point, what will the police perceive when they come on the scene? How will they know you are the victim, not the assailant? The gun in your hand marks you as a threat of some kind. You can avoid a mistaken-identity shooting by discretely holstering the gun the moment before the law officers come through the door. The rigid, open top allows you to holster the gun without looking, so you can keep your eyes on the assailant at all times. Recent developments in rigid nylon holsters have offered several synthetic holsters that look like they will

Smith & Wesson's Model 640, a snub-nosed .38 Special, rides comfortably at the hip in a Milt Sparks Summer Special belt holster.

equal the performance of leather gear. You should, in any case, *insist* that the holster remain open at the top when the gun is withdrawn.

Orca Custom International, a Washington State manufacturer, makes a very comfortable rigid nylon holster, the "Grand Master," that sits

Smith & Wesson's 9mm Model 3913, carried in an Orca holster, is one of the easiest semi-automatics to conceal comfortably.

low inside the waistband. Lots of men's holsters ride too high for women, who generally have shorter torsos than men. A high-ride holster that fits a man perfectly will put the butt of the gun at armpit level on most women, making it nearly impossible to draw the gun.

Some holsters come equipped to accommodate several widths of belts. My Milt Sparks Executive Companion, for instance, has two screws that attach the belt loop to the holster. A smaller loop is sold for 1-inch belts and costs $7.50, which I gladly spent, knowing I had pants and skirts that wouldn't accommodate my inch-and-a-half gun belt. And speaking of belts, your common dress belt isn't going to last long under the weight of your gun and holster. Budget $25 to $40 for a good gun belt produced by a reputable holster manufacturer. The belt should be thick, but need not be stiff. I used a 1-3/8" Safariland belt with casual pants for a long time. It has a thicker leather outer layer stitched to soft suede leather on the inside. It is very pliable and formed to my body shape right away. I then received a handsome Bianchi smooth leather belt that looks a little more fashionable with dressier clothing. The brand's not as important as its ability to support your gun and holster.

Choose a good quality leather holster from a reputable manufacturer. Readily available choices include Bianchi, Galco, and DeSantis. Spend a few more dollars and you can have the unequaled design and workmanship of Milt Sparks, Greg Kramer, or Ted Blocker.

A second holster—something like buying a red purse after you have one in a neutral color—might include a shoulder holster or an ankle holster.

Shoulder holsters

Like inside-the-waistband holsters, shoulder rigs come in all sizes and designs, and hang the pistol in all sorts of directions. If you feel squeamish about having a pistol pointed at your left arm pit, gravitate toward the downward pointing shoulder holster or a rig that orients the gun horizontally, muzzle pointing past your back. Many slender people find the horizontal carry allows the gun muzzle to poke out behind the armpit, thus announcing its presence. The largest I could hope to completely conceal in the horizontal position is a .38 snubby.

One of the nicest large shoulder holsters is a vertical muzzle-down holster from Bianchi (Model X-88) dubbed, "The Sting." It is built around a heavy-duty spring-steel clip that keeps the pistol firmly in place. After verifying that the safety is engaged, the shooter inserts the gun muzzle first, then pivots the frame of the gun to open the rest of that spring-steel frame to accept the slide or barrel. I won my M-88 in an IPSC stock gun match, and found that adjusting it was as difficult as

Kramer holster made of horsehide.

lacing Scarlett O'Hara into her corset. This is no job to tackle single handedly or with someone with whom you are not willing to be quite intimate. Adjusting numerous nylon straps took considerable time, and becoming accustomed to the feel of the rig took longer.

My friend Jane, who introduced me to the wonderful Milt Sparks Executive Companion inside-the-waistband holster carries her Glock in the traditional position, behind her strong side hip. She is taller and has a smaller waistline than I, and her gun conceals comfortably in that position. Nonetheless, the last time I saw Jane, on a humid July day in western Washington, she was toting a .38 Special in a belly bag holster pouch. Hot weather will be a determining factor in how you carry your gun. I also concede to shorts weather by tucking my semi-automatic

Galco's premium "Executive" shoulder holster hides a Walther PPK .380 beneath even a soft sweater. This beautiful holster is easy to adjust and comfortable from the first wearing.

into a specially designed belly bag sometimes. I prefer nylon to leather, since it has a more "normal" appearance. Some holster fanny packs have wide Velcro® straps to secure the gun, an elastic band to hold an extra magazine in place, plus a cord for a downward rip to open the carry pouch and expose the gun for the draw. Others have a built-in holster attached to the back panel of the bag.

Choices include Bianchi's roomy nylon pouch with side pockets, an unusual detail I appreciated. I like a small pocket to serve exclusively as magazine pouch or place to tuck pistol permits and identification papers or other objects I don't want mixed with other things. DeSantis was the original designer to use Velcro® on belly-bag pockets, a design they've patented. I prefer their Gunnysack II, an extremely well-designed belly bag with a full rip-away front panel that reliably exposes the holstered gun for a fast draw.

Other hot weather alternatives include the belly band—traditionally made of wide elastic, re-introduced in 1991 in a feminine version, complete with lace and designed to be worn around the midriff/rib-cage. For comfort, however, my choice is a band made of soft surgical elastic sold by Doctor Center. Bianchi makes a plainer version, as does Gould & Goodrich.

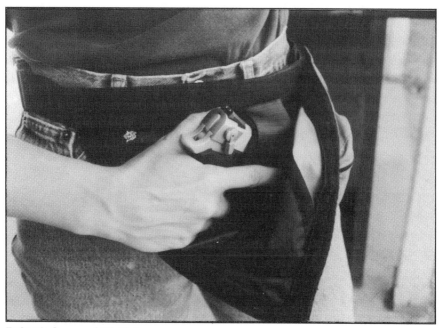

DeSantis Gunnysack® belly bag.

Gould & Goodrich also makes a wide elastic belt that works on the same principle, designed to be worn outside the clothing, with a false buckle on the front. Tucked beneath a blazer or sweater, the Gould & Goodrich Lady Bodyguard looks like a wide fashion belt. The gun is positioned at or behind the hip, in a sewn-in holster-shaped enclosure with a Velcro®-secured thumb strap to make sure the gun stays in place. It works great with guns like a .38 air weight revolver or the .380 semi-automatic Walther PPK, but with sufficiently concealing garments, will accommodate small semi-autos like the S&W 3913. I use my Lady Bodyguard for all-day seminars or trade shows, where a blazer and skirt are *de rigeur*. I can virtually forget the air weight Smith & Wesson Model 642 revolver the belt holds securely at my hip.

Thigh holsters are like the belly-band—try it if nothing else works with the clothing you must wear. Suspended from a waistband on garter-like straps, the thigh holster will secure a small frame gun on the inside of your thigh. I cannot vouch for the comfort or discomfort of this arrangement, since I rarely have to wear dresses and favor a belly band or shoulder holster for use with skirts and suit jackets.

I like to break in a holster by wearing it around the house so I can adjust or move the holster if it becomes uncomfortable. A new holster, worn immediately in public, can inflict considerable discomfort. I'd rather find out where it rubs and where it needs to be adjusted in the privacy of my own quarters before I wear the thing on the street. I also recommend several hundred "dry" repetitions of drawing the un-loaded gun from the holster, assuming a shooting stance, and dry firing, when breaking in a new holster.

The body, medical folks tell us, needs 2,000 to 5,000 repetitions of any movement before it becomes automatic. Remember when driving a manual transmission car was nearly impossible? Now, if you drive that kind of car regularly, shifting is as automatic as brushing your teeth. After around 5,000 repetitions, drawing and firing your handgun becomes natural, too. You can get a good start on those repetitive movements by practicing with an unloaded gun. Skills to develop include a fumble-free draw, but be sure none of your motions allows the gun muzzle to cross any part of your body during the draw.

Practice with any holster or gun must be accomplished with the weapon unloaded. Put all the ammunition in a box or drawer in a different room. Double check to see that the chamber or cylinder is empty. Learning your safe way around your new holster will take some time and practice. Drill in complete privacy, without distractions or the danger of inadvertently pointing your gun at a family member. Refer to the "Dryfire" section in Shooting Skills, Chapter 18, for safe, productive practice routines.

Gould & Goodrich's Lady Bodyguard holds the author's S&W 3913 easily. A blazer will cover the gun completely, for wear in public.

Ankle holsters

Men do have it easier in a few regards. Not only do men's rest room lines move faster, men don't have to give birth, and they can wear ankle holsters with nearly all of their trousers! An ankle holster is one of the hardest-to-detect modes of concealed carry, one my husband takes advantage of for his backup .38. I'm always a little jealous as I watch him tuck his .38 air weight into an ankle rig concealed by his dark dress socks.

Women *can* use an ankle holster, although with more selectivity. Most of our jeans and slacks are cut slim at the ankle, immediately disqualifying much of our wardrobe from use with an ankle holster. Buy wide-legged trousers that are cut straight from thigh to hem. These are often nice-looking pleated chinos or lined dress slacks. An inch or two of extra length at the hemline will assure that when you sit, the trouser leg will not ride up and reveal your weapon tucked on the inside your leg, right above the ankle bone. A pair of sweat pants with gathered, elasticized cuffs hides an ankle rig best of all.

Drawing your weapon from an ankle holster requires practice. The right-handed "defender" takes a big step, left-leg forward. The left hand grabs a handful of trouser leg on the thigh above the knee, where the hand can rest and support the weight as the right hand snakes down and snatches the gun from its holster inside the left ankle. The defender then simply straightens the torso and is ready to shoot. The feet are already in an aggressive shooting stance. If the pants are too tight to grab and lift, drop to the non-gun knee, grab the pistol and shoot from a high kneeling position.

Holster purses

I'm quite uncomfortable with a gun carried off the body, but reality takes its toll on idealism, and I have to admit that there are times when a purse or bag is the only real option for keeping a gun in easy reach. At a dress-up affair, a woman carrying a nice leather handbag is inconspicuous, but a woman who cannot take off her jacket can become pretty uncomfortable. I concede: a gun purse is a good solution under some circumstances.

Some will ask why they can't put the gun in their normal handbag. There are several very good reasons for avoiding this foolishness. The first is the presence of other objects that become caught in and foul the gun's action, or worse yet, may knock the gun's safety off and allow it to be fired negligently. This is not just a problem for amateurs. I was recently at a conference of the American Society of Law Enforcement Trainers, and listened in amazement as a trainer described the tribulations of an off-duty female law enforcement officer who drew a revolver from her purse to find an eyebrow pencil jammed down the barrel.

The second reason for using a purse designed to carry a gun is ease of draw. Pulling a weapon from a conventional handbag will be a terribly slow affair, as the defender fumbles with the latch or zipper, then dredges through the other personal effects trying to find the weapon. A gun purse has a center pouch that is inaccessible from the rest of the bag, often with a sewn-in holster to hold the gun in the same position all the time. To draw, insert your hand, grasp the butt and present the weapon in a cross-draw manner. If the gun purse does not have a dedicated pouch and a built-in holster, don't purchase it. There are plenty of very good ones that have both features, including some very fast and positive designs that make getting to the gun in an emergency fast and fumble-free.

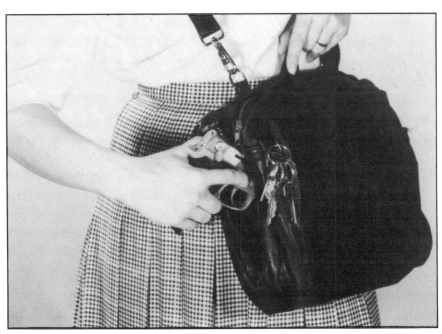

Guardian Leather's business portfolio.

The best fast-draw design I've seen is the two-compartment bag from DeSantis. This gun purse looks like a conventional woman's handbag. The front section holds your personal goods; the back section is large enough to contain a medium-sized semi-automatic (or anything smaller). The weight of the personal effects causes that front compartment to drop like a stone when pulled downward to expose the rear compartment and the weapon. The draw from this bag is very similar to the up-and-out draw of a conventional inside-the-waistband holster, and therefore is considerably faster than bags that tuck the gun horizontally in a center section between two pockets.

For business events, I've been very happy with the handsome portfolio marketed by Guardian Leather. It has two large pockets for papers and books, and a hidden compartment in the middle for your gun. With this design, the woman reaches cross body, separates the Velcro® closure, grabs the gun butt and makes a cross-body draw. This takes some practice, and is a few seconds slower than DeSantis' excellent design. Velcro® tabs secure a holster sized to fit your gun, making it easy to change the hol-

Drawing from DeSantis "Executive," shown on the cover.

ster if you decide to carry different guns in the bag. I ordered two holsters—one for the Glock and one for a .38 Special, but in a bag this size, it seems ridiculous not to carry the higher capacity, bigger caliber Glock, since it fits in the bag just as easily as a .38 Special. Really, the only constraining factor is the weight you can carry on your shoulder. I find the fully loaded Glock 23 with spare magazine is just about the maximum for me, and my shoulder is sore after long business days. Guardian Leather also makes a little clutch that will take your .38 Special or small .380 semi-auto to evening soirees and fashionable events, as does Galco.

Some of the most fashionable bags are coming from the hands of Sarah LaPere of Feminine Protection. She combines different materials and attractive colors for a nice variety of gun bags. Some models have straps that can be replaced with pretty gold chain straps for a dressier look.

The greatest difficulty I have in justifying gun purses is the question of proper response to a purse snatching. Experts agree that the best response to muggers or purse snatchers is to give them the purse or wallet, so long as the woman is allowed to escape unharmed. Run-by purse snatching can turn into an ugly ground fight on the pavement if

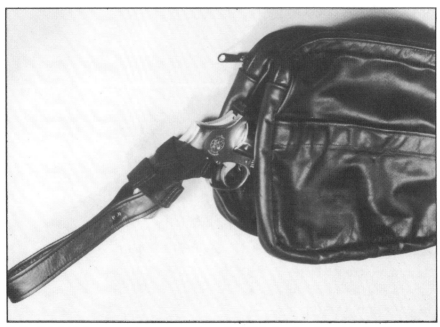

DeSantis' clutch has a gun-strap to prevent gun theft if the handbag is snatched on the street.

the woman struggles to keep her bag. Advice to give up a snatched bag is drastically altered by the presence of a deadly weapon in the purse. We know we must not use deadly force to stop property theft, yet we also know we must keep our gun out of criminal hands.

The best decision is to use the holster purse only in social or business circumstances that do not take you out on busy city sidewalks. If unexpected circumstances put you at risk of purse snatchings, carry the bag cross-body, the strap on the shoulder opposite the side the bag hangs on and tuck that bag in tight to the front of your body where the savvy criminal knows it is more difficult to grab. Try other holster methods, including shoulder and ankle holsters before falling back on holster bags for every day use.

If you decide to tuck a gun into a handbag—one specially designed for a gun—you must be committed to keeping that purse on your body or between your ankles at all times. A purse hung off the back of a chair is subject to theft or investigation by a small child. Neither is acceptable when the purse contains a gun. A purse left on a host's coat tree or couch is also accessible to unauthorized hands. The gun is a serious responsibility. If you aren't willing to keep it with you at *all times*, you must leave it safely locked away.

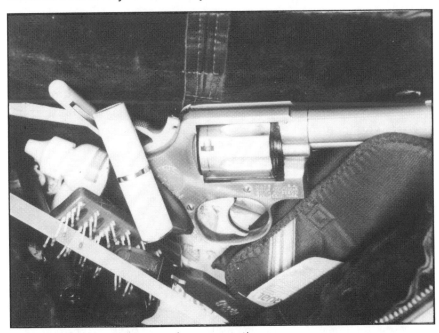

A gun in a regular handbag is a very dangerous practice.

Clothing for concealed carry

A cute 25-year old student complained that carrying a gun really wasn't possible. She didn't like the feel of a fanny pack, but she liked to wear her jeans really tight, she said. An in-the-waistband concealment holster wouldn't fit, she had concluded. The question sounded like a challenge: "tell me how to carry my gun with no hassle, and then I'll agree with your advice to carry it all the time." Fortunately, there was a good answer for this one: if you want to show off your figure, buy boys or men's jeans—they still fit tight in the rear, but they're cut roomier through the waist to accommodate a holster and gun.

A lot of armed people find themselves buying their wardrobes around the gun. We select pants that have a little extra room in the waist. Our trousers have waistbands with belt loops for a sturdy belt and straight, loose legs to hide ankle holsters. We buy blazers that are more loosely fitted to hide either an in-the-waistband or shoulder holster. Others have adopted the casual photographer or fisherman's vest to hide the gun, or wear oversized shirts over tank tops in the summertime.

It's not really as much trouble as it seems in the beginning. After a while, fitting the gun into your clothing style becomes as natural as making sure you have white underwear to wear with white slacks.

First holster choices

Holster selection can be a confusing job for the new gun owner. At the very beginning, the individual might be best served by obtaining an inexpensive nylon belt holster for training, a belly bag for summer, or gun purse for formal events. As your advancing classes and training prepare you for armed self defense situations, go shopping for a good leather holster with a rigid, open top. You'll need to budget between $60 and $100 for this chore, but with your advancing skill you will recognize the tactical advantage a good holster offers for both conceal- ment and for drawing the gun.

Sources for products shown in this chapter:

Kramer Handgun Leather, P.O. Box 112154, Tacoma, WA 98411 (206) 564-5740.
Bianchi International, 100 Calle Cortez, Temecula, CA 92590 (800) 477-8545.
DeSantis, P.O. Box 2039, Hillside Manor Branch, New Hyde Park, NY 11040 (516) 354-8000.
Guardian Leather, P.O. Box 277, Newton Centre, MA 02159 (617) 527-1819.
Milt Sparks Holsters Inc., 605 E. 44th, #2, Boise, ID 82714 (208) 377-5577.
Orca Custom International, Inc., P.O. Box 330, Winlock, WA 98596 (206) 785-3885.
Gould & Goodrich, P.O. Box 1479, Lillington, NC 27546 (919) 893-2071.
Doctor Center, 4244 Main Ave., Baldwin Park, Dept. F, CA 91706 (800) 442-3627.
Feminine Protection, 10514 Shady Trail, Dallas, TX 75220 (800) 444-7090.

17
Tactics to Survive What You Can't Avoid

We've discussed the importance of avoiding trouble, but must still be prepared for dangers that we can't avoid. Having a handgun doesn't make the danger go away—it only provides a tool that helps you control danger, much as a fire extinguisher gives you the chance to stop a fire before your house burns down. John and Vicki Farnam taught, reinforced, and clarified my grasp of handgun tactics. Their influence will be apparent in the pages that follow.

The most difficult decision comes in the moment between recognizing the threat and deciding if it is a lethal assault. Caught by a mugger, it's best to keep a safe distance and toss over your wallet. The legal and

John and Vicki Farnam coach the author and a fellow student during a class drill.

emotional aftermath of a shooting far exceeds the loss of the cash you are carrying. However, if an assailant charges at you yelling, "Hey, bitch, I'm gonna really mess you up," you need to react to a crippling assault, not a robbery. This set of tactics is different than verbal intervention or avoidance.

Because entertainment is obsessed with violence, we see thousands of portrayals of victimization—assaults on innocents who are raped or murdered because they had no defensive plan, skill or weapon. I believe women are being *trained* by television to be victims, while men are being trained to be victimizers. As you watch the repeated television scenes of men assaulting woman, mentally envision an appropriate response from the victim: imagine how *you* would respond. Decide now that you *will* cause injury to avoid being hurt. Prepare your mind to survive, to direct your body to fight off an assault.

Mental preparation comes from making *The Decision*. Training with your weapon and planning what you would do if faced with a violent assailant prepares your body to respond automatically when your mind recognizes an assault. Those who have not trained and planned to fight off a lethal assault freeze in terror or react hysterically, unable to mount a counter-attack. Defense training teaches defensive skills. Practice and repetition ingrain them in the muscle memory so the body can respond to attack without step-by-step direction from the mind.

In the discussion of rape, I find it disturbing that victims and those who counsel women on survival tactics talk about the kinds of injury women are *willing to endure*. A story coming from the southern states tells of a woman who, during the course of her abduction, chose not to use a revolver she carried in her purse. She determined she could endure the rape, and it was not until the rapist turned from sexual to lethal assault that she decided she could not accept death, drew her gun, and killed the man. She was fortunate, if you can call it that. She experienced extreme emotional repercussions, including months of immobilizing fear in which she was unable to leave her bedroom. She bore the condemnation of a small town that sympathized with a dead assailant and believed the lies of his family; and went through a legal nightmare, defending her decision to kill the murderous rapist.

And yet, I do believe she was fortunate. Many who do not fight off an assailant from the first indication of lethal assault lose the thin edge that firm tactical control of the situation might have given them. They perish.

The first step of tactical readiness is your determination not to be a victim. Decide that from the first indication of danger you will fight. Making that determination should lead to a decision to get good training, not just in how to shoot, but in threat management and survival skills, too.

Survival tactics

The first rule of survival is controlling the distance between you and the assailant. Against contact weapons like bludgeons and knives, the distance you can create to escape or draw your own weapon determines your survival. Protective cover against contact weapons consists of obstacles that impede your attacker. If the threat is made with a firearm, you must protect yourself behind bullet-stopping cover. Protective cover is often confused with concealment. A sheet rock wall provides concealment, but it will not stop a bullet. In taking cover, we have to find objects dense enough to impede a bullet.

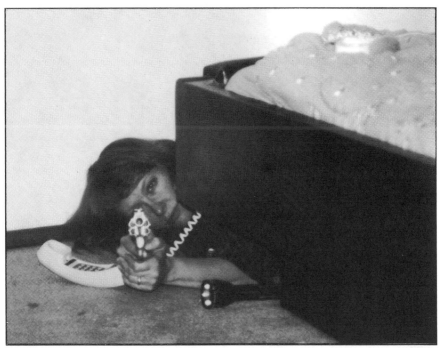

In the bedroom a water bed offers concealment and bullet stopping cover. Taking cover also means reducing the size of target you present, as seen here.

Develop a cover-conscious mindset. Look around in restaurants, walking down sidewalks, in department stores and banks. Try to recognize objects that would stop bullets. Envision crouching behind the cover. Could you return fire without endangering other innocents? In the home, you should shield yourself behind heavy furniture like a solidly filled bookcase, then expose only the arms and only as much of the head as necessary to aim your gun at the assailant's chest. If nothing else is available, even the lumber in a door frame is preferable to full body exposure.

If attacked on the street, cars, large trees, buildings and other natural objects provide some safety in which to hunker down and return fire. If you use a car, crouch behind the engine block for best bullet-stopping protection. You will read that few handgun bullets can penetrate a car door. Films of law enforcement agencies shooting up old 1960s vintage cars, show few bullets penetrating to strike a paper dummy in the driver's seat. On the other hand, I watched John Farnam fire several .45 caliber bullets in one door and out the opposite door of a VW Rabbit, and although this excellent instructor emphasizes the limited power of handgun ammunition, the light construction of modern automobiles can't

If you must shoot from behind cover, roll only enough of your body out to identify the target and shoot, then duck back behind cover. When you roll out again, come out at a different height or position, so the assailant can't guess your position and shoot you as you pop out.

162

be trusted to stop a bullet. I, for one, don't care to test any ballistic theory with my body.

The trouble with crouching behind the bulk of the engine block is that the only way to return fire is to rise and expose your head and shoulders as you take aim and shoot. When possible, find a heavy wall to get behind. In extremely exposed conditions, employ utility poles, large trees, concrete abutments and other heavy fixtures to protect your body's central mass.

If you shoot from behind cover at an assailant, avoid predictable actions that the assailant can second-guess. If you repeatedly peek out in a full standing position, he can simply approximate the height you last appeared at, line up his gun sights on that spot, and shoot you as you appear to take your next shot. Instead, if the cover is vertical, take a shot from full standing, drop to a crouch for the next shot, and so forth. Behind horizontal cover, scuttle from side to side keeping your assailant off guard and confused.

When using cover, especially outdoors, remember the vulnerable area behind your line of vision. Don't be so focused on the assailant in front

A car's engine block and wheels can provide bullet stopping cover. Don't remain exposed: pop up to take your shot then duck behind the car so you will not be shot.

of your gun that you forget he may have a companion approaching from behind. During lulls in the action, reload and take a 360° danger scan to be sure nothing else is approaching from other directions. You have to consciously fight the natural compulsion to tunnel in on the perceived source of danger. This is one of the tachypsychia effects addressed in the third chapter. John and Vicki Farnam teach their students to physically turn their heads, looking left and looking right, after a stress drill. They believe the physical activity helps break up the tunnel vision that always accompanies a lethal assault.

On the move

If your assailant moves or an accomplice approaches, you will have to leave the relative safety of your bookcase, brick wall, or engine block, and move to a different place of cover. This is no time to imitate the movies, where a gunman makes his way stealthily down a hall, gun muzzle pointing upwards. This is a good time to mimic a jackrabbit dashing across a busy highway. At this moment, your future is as questionable as the road kill's.

Locate a different source of cover, then sprint to it. During movement, take your finger out of the trigger guard. It doesn't belong on the trigger unless you *have your gun raised and aimed at a target you may have to shoot.* The stress and activity of your dash could cause a negligent discharge. Don't point the gun skyward, as also "taught" in the movies. In urban situations, particularly, the responsibility for all your bullets equals the safety of innocent people who live nearby. Keep both hands on the grip, and pull the gun in tight to your body. This low ready position denies the gun to an assailant who may grab it, but keeps it instantly ready. In this position, a close range shot is as fast as thrusting the gun into your line of vision, seeing it silhouetted against your target and pulling the trigger.

The same technique is advisable if, ignoring all advice, you have decided to go through the house searching for the source of a disturbing noise. Find a safe place where you can't be flanked to survey the area for danger. When satisfied that the area is clear, move rapidly to the next cover, gun tucked in close to your body. When approaching doors, if you believe the area behind you is free of threat, remain on the outside, and roll out your head and a minimum of torso to peek quickly into the next room. Sound terrifying? It ought to. Clearing a house of dangerous intruders is better left to a trained police team and their canine assistants.

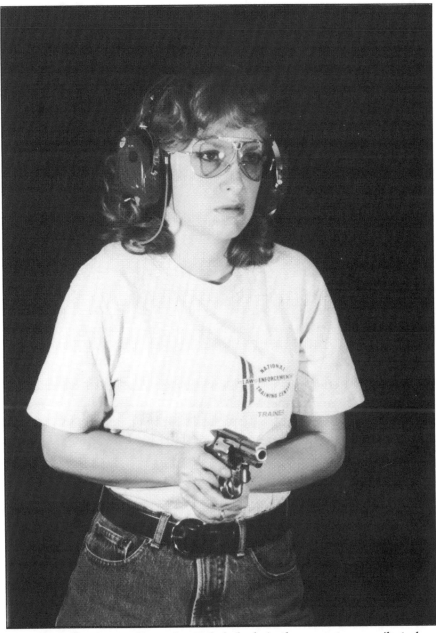

The ready position, keeping the gun close to the body, denies the weapon to an assailant who may try to grab it.

Close encounters

If you face an assailant who has a drawn gun, don't try to draw your own in response. His advantage is too great. He can shoot you before your gun ever leaves the holster. Even a respectable two second draw can't beat a gun already in the hands of an assailant. There are several lessons here; the first to extend the distance and take cover whenever possible. At face-to-face distances, you're basically staring death in the eyes unless you have learned handgun retention and disarming techniques. An element in some disarm techniques is to start talking to the assailant, distracting him from your intent to take away the weapon. John Farnam writes that speaking first gives you an air of self-assurance and gives a bit of a psychological edge, letting the assailant know that although you face his handgun, you are not frightened into immobility. Later in this chapter we'll discuss the downside of talking in a self defense situation.

Faced with multiple assailants, you should neutralize the closest, most immediate threat first. Don't take a long time to analyze: make it an ingrained, pre-planned response to shoot the closest assailant, then move the front sight to center on the next closest person or the one that clearly poses the greatest threat. With practice, the shooter can move from one target to another with smoothness and control. Practiced on three or four targets in a row, the shooter fires the first shot, and instead of regaining the sight picture on the same target, lets the recoil move the sights onto the next target, fires the next shot, and lets the recoil move the front sight to the next target. If the last assailants break off and flee, you must let them go. To shoot a retreating criminal is not necessary, moral, or legal. As a fight is broken off, be it against one or several assailants, scan the nearby area to be sure there are no other assailants closing in.

A gunfight may require more than one magazine or cylinder-full of ammunition, especially if the handgun is a low-capacity compact semi-automatic or a revolver. Inexperienced shooters claim they would count their shots in a gunfight, so they won't have to reload. That is the voice of naiveté and inexperience. Under the stress of a lethal encounter, no one, no matter how experienced or hardened, has the presence of mind to count the shots they've fired.

Jim Cirillo, once with New York's police department and later a firearms trainer for the Federal Law Enforcement Training Center, relates that even police officers shoot their guns "dry" from time to time. In one case, the officer was a mere fourteen or fifteen feet away from the felon. Both men emptied their guns at each other, missed, and both found themselves pulling the trigger on an empty gun. "The guns were just going click, click," Cirillo relates. The officer began to search in his pocket for ammunition and came up with car keys, a nickel and a dime, which he attempted to load, duplicating the police range procedure of placing the ammunition in the pocket. The officer became flustered, and when he remembered that his ammunition was in a pouch on the belt, fumbled and spilled the rounds on the ground. When the officer knelt to retrieve the ammunition, the felon rushed him. Several rounds were already chambered, and the officer closed the cylinder and began pulling the trigger. After several pulls, the loaded chambers lined up and the officer was able to put several bullets into the attacker's chest at close range.

Much of the time, the indication that the gun is empty comes when there is no response to pulling the trigger, or is signaled by a locked-back slide on a semi-automatic. In any case, protective cover would be a darn nice thing to have when it's time to take that two to ten seconds out of the fight to reload your gun. Prior practice reloading could make the difference between survival and dying at the hands of a freely advancing assailant.

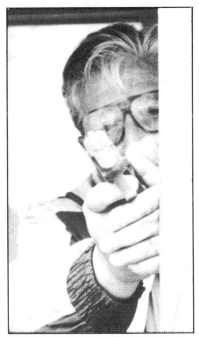

The foremost rule of gun fighting is to *shoot no faster than you can hit the target.* In view of the physical fight-or-flight adrenaline rush that takes place in an emergency, it's not surprising that in encounters involving police officers and criminals, only a fraction of the bullets fired hit the target. Unfortunately, only the bullets that hit can help stop the danger. Your sights must be lined up on the center of the assailant's chest. In most cases, several, perhaps many, shots will be required to stop the assailant.

Jim Cirillo teaches shooting from behind cover at a class the author attended.

Television mis-informs and mis-trains us to expect one handgun bullet to spin an assailant off his feet and halfway across the room. In his informative book, *Handgun Stopping Power*, Evan Marshall relates an incident where a fighter took seven or eight rounds of .45 ball ammunition in the torso, then caught a city bus to the nearest hospital. Could this person have continued a killing assault if he had wished? Absolutely. Leaving behind the anachronism of .45 ball ammunition, Evan cites case after case of assailants continuing to fight after taking multiple hits of 9mm, .45, or .357 caliber hollowpoint ammunition. You must condition yourself to continue to fire your defense handgun *until the threat ceases*.

If several center-of-mass shots have failed to deter an advancing assailant, consider aiming the next shot at the pelvis. This large bone is integral to the body's structure, and breaking it will drop him to the ground. If the assailant is holding a gun, however, you cannot consider a downed assailant no longer dangerous. You have only taken his mobility, not his ability to shoot.

Instant stops are difficult to achieve, requiring very exactly placed shots to the brain's medulla oblongata at the base of the skull. The brain can also be accessed by exact shots through the eye sockets, or with less probability, through the mouth. At any tactically-safe distance, achieving this level of marksmanship under high-stress conditions is very difficult. Head shots should be attempted only to instantly drop a hostage-taker, where the situation requires an instant stop to save the hostage. This is a job for SWAT snipers, not citizens armed with short-barreled self defense pistols.

Advice to shoot merely to frighten or wound an assailant is dangerously wrong. The amateurs giving that advice recommend, "just hurt the criminal," implying that shooting his legs is more justifiable than employing deadly force. The act of firing a gun at a human being *is* employing lethal force, regardless of your aim point. By firing, you have just escalated an argument, robbery, or other lesser crime into a gun fight. Don't misunderstand: you need not and should not wait for him to fire the first shot. However, if *you* decide to fire, be completely certain that you are in immediate and unavoidable danger of death or crippling injury, then shoot to vital areas to stop the threat that caused you to draw the weapon in the first place. Never fire unless you believe your life or the life of another is at risk.

What else have you done by firing a warning shot? You have told your assailant that he is facing a gun without a determined human behind it. He will either advance and take your gun, or draw his own and shoot you down, knowing you cannot bring yourself to kill. Finally, you are responsible for injury your warning shot may cause another person. Remember, handgun bullets can pass through wood, windows, and other barriers.

A street assailant follows no rules of engagement. Your confirmation of danger may be a punch that knocks you flat on your back. This scenario is an excellent argument against small-of-the-back holsters and a warning to learn physical skills to recover from being knocked down, as well as shooting from a variety of positions. Some will say you should be able to draw while on the ground and blast away, and indeed training and practicing from both supine and prone positions is advisable. I think it makes more tactical sense to learn to fall and roll out of your assailant's reach. Martial arts, as an adjunct to handguns, again proves valuable. Training halls have mats to break the fall, and any good school can teach students how to fall without injury, and how to roll up and regain their balance, as well as teaching good kicks and traps to execute from the ground with feet and legs.

Firing from a fallen position may be mandated if you have been injured in the fight. Jim Cirillo teaches prone firing as part of his Downed Officer Survival Course. In extreme, close-in assaults, one would simply line up the sights on the assailant and pull the trigger. At greater distances the gun can be braced atop or between the drawn-up knees as the body contracts into a fetal position. I found the braced-gun positions extremely accurate, if somewhat slow.

Surviving a gunshot wound

If you are hit with a bullet, continue to fire on your assailant. Remember that very few handgun wounds are immediately lethal. What *will* prove lethal is if you stop firing on your assailant, and let him walk up and fire a bullet directly into your head. Ignore the fear, ignore the blood or pain, and center your front sight on the assailant's chest and keep pressing the trigger for controlled, rapid fire. When the assault stops, check your wounds, apply pressure where needed and get medical attention.

If your bullet fells an assailant, don't assume that he is incapacitated. You must maintain your distance, and preferably stay behind cover, while taking control of the situation. People who have been hit by handgun bullets report the initial sensation was like taking a hard punch with a fist. Under the fight-or-flight adrenaline rush, they often do not realize they've been shot until later, when the blood draws their attention to the gunshot wound.

Controlling an assailant

Check the assailant's hands for weapons that he could use to renew the assault. Do not approach a fallen assailant; do not attempt to tie him or restrain him. This is still a dangerous human who wishes you harm. *Do* have your gun's safety *off* with the weapon ready to fire in double action mode. Single action weapons should be on-safe, with the thumb riding atop the safety for a quick flick into "fire" mode. Keep your gun fixed on the assailant. Keep your finger outside the trigger guard, to avoid a startle response that might make you unintentionally fire the gun. This is a time for control; you don't want a negligent discharge of the gun to allow his heirs to charge that you "finished him off" after he no longer posed a threat.

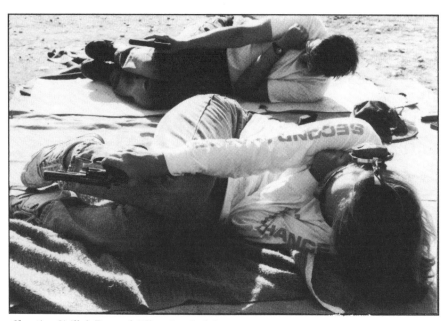

Shooting Cirillo's Downed Officer Survival Course.

Don't let the assailant engage you in conversation; limit your communication with him to brief, forceful commands. Short, sharp syllables elicit obedience while minimizing the amount of time your nervous system is occupied with the speech act. Humans are capable of only limited simultaneous activity. It is nearly impossible to continue coherent speech and fire a handgun at the same time. I have engaged in training routines with dummy guns, taking role-playing "assailants" at dummy-gun point. One of the most revealing lessons came when I ordered the assailant to assume a hands-above-head position. While I completed the command, the "assailants" drew their dummy gun and "shot" me. I found myself incapable of returning fire until I had finished the sentence. Stress causes motor mouth, so we need to memorize a very brief order of commands.

Delivered in command voice, emanating forcefully from the diaphragm, the commands are brief and explosive. The first:
   "Don't move!"
when forcefully delivered has the psychic force to bring action to a temporary standstill. Then:
   "Drop that weapon!"
is the next command if you see a gun, knife or bludgeon in his hands. If not, it may be appropriate to command,
   "Don't touch that weapon!"
Assuming he intends to draw a weapon he carries, improvise a bludgeon from any object he can reach, or grab for your drawn handgun you would now command:
   "Slowly, raise your hands."
If you find you must put an assailant in a controllable posture, order him to take slow, controlled movements that you can monitor. Keep any movements you order slow and controlled. Deny any opportunity for the assailant to rapidly turn and renew his assault on you. With his hands at waist level, an assailant can quickly pull a gun from his belt and fire before you have time to react.

What then follows, as taught at Lethal Force Institute, are orders to slowly turn face away from you, kneel, cross ankles and slowly drop to the floor, lying face down with hands and arms fully extended. Know where his hands are at all times. Keep distance and objects between you to increase your zone of safety against a surprise attack. When he is prone and facing away from you, you can scan the area for accomplices, reach for a nearby telephone, and dial 911. At the last moment, you can

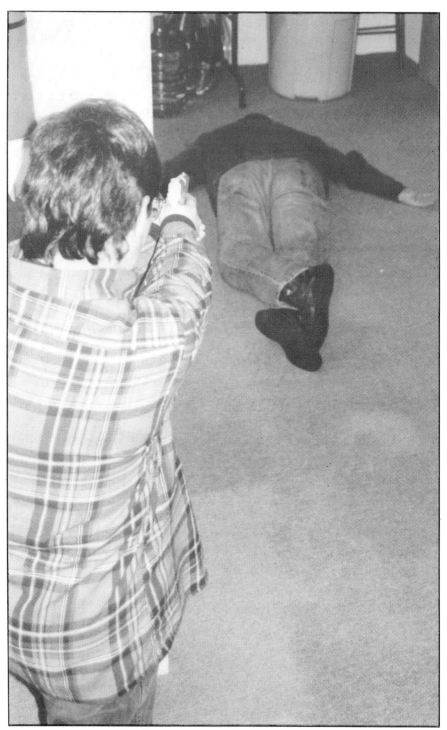

Statistics show that civilians scare off or hold criminals for police more often than they actually shoot. Learning how to take a house-breaker at gun point could prove very valuable.

safely holster your own weapon before the police come through the door.

Further discussion of holding an assailant at gun point appears in *In The Gravest Extreme*, by Massad Ayoob, also an excellent source for tactical information. Formal training in handgun tactics is essential for the person who carries a gun for self defense. Lethal Force Institute or instructors trained by Ayoob, and John and Vicki Farnam are all excellent sources of training. Additional written material recommended is Farnam's *The Street Smart Gun Book*.[1]

Having practiced and thought out what you would do if assailed under varying circumstances is valuable. As John and Vicki Farnam are fond of saying during their training courses, "Have a plan." Pre-determine how you would respond if a knife wielder rushed at you on a crowded street. Think about how you would react in a deserted street at midnight if approached by a threatening person. See the images in your mind. Feel your body ready to make the appropriate response.

---

[1] *In the Gravest Extreme* and *The Street Smart Gun Book* are published by Police Bookshelf, P.O. Box 122, Concord, NH 03301.

18
Shooting Skills

Earlier we discussed obtaining basic handgun training and understanding appropriate use of deadly force. Discussing tactics, we emphasized the importance of accurate shot placement. Marksmanship skills are just the beginning; your training needs to include drills that teach you to shoot accurately and rapidly under great stress. Self defense shootings entail fear and surprise, with one or more targets that move and intend to harm you.

In basic handgun class you should have learned about sight picture, follow-through, and trigger control. To reiterate anything you may have forgotten, here is an overview of the three basics.

Sight picture

The handgun has two sighting devices to help you line up the barrel on your target. The front sight is generally a blade with a dot or colored insert to help you focus. The rear sight is shaped like a shallow "U" and may have two dots or a bright outline around the notch to help clarify the edges. If the front sight is perfectly centered in the notch of the rear sight and the top of both sights are perfectly aligned, *the bullet will hit the target where the front sight points when the gun fires.*

As I bring the gun up on the target I see three objects: the rear sight, the front sight and the target beyond. If I see the target clearly, both sights are fuzzy. If I focus on the rear sight, anything beyond it is blurry. Our eyes can focus on only one visual plane at a time. *We must concentrate on the front sight* to be sure our sights remain aligned and that the front sight centers on the point we wish the bullet to enter. On paper targets, or facing a human assailant, it is natural to want to look at the object we need to shoot. That is a recipe for disaster because attention on the target allows the front sight to wander all over the place and inevitably causes inaccurate shooting. Focus your attention on the front sight as if it holds your life and your future. It may.

Trigger squeeze

A smooth, consistent pressure on the trigger is the key to accurate shooting. Jerking or stabbing at the trigger moves the sights out of alignment, so the shot goes wild. Experienced drivers press the car brake pedal smoothly until they bring the vehicle to a stop. That same smoothness is what you want from your trigger finger. A deliberate four second trigger squeeze starts with up to two seconds of smooth controlled pull on the trigger. At some point between two and four seconds, the gun fires without you knowing exactly when it was going to go "bang!" The remaining second is dedicated to follow-through— bringing the gun back on target, lining up the sights perfectly, and instantly assessing the situation to see if you need to shoot again.

The same consistent trigger press, surprise shot, and follow through can be compressed to under a second per shot. Consistent pressure on

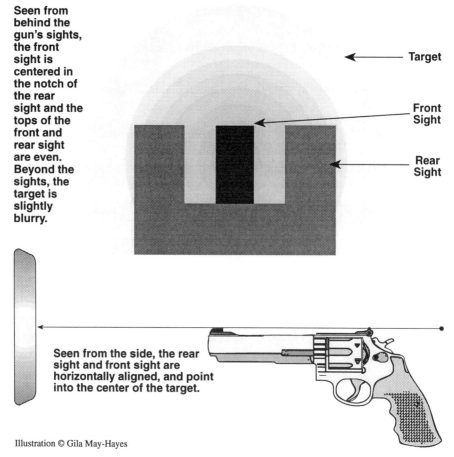

Seen from behind the gun's sights, the front sight is centered in the notch of the rear sight and the tops of the front and rear sight are even. Beyond the sights, the target is slightly blurry.

Target

Front Sight

Rear Sight

Seen from the side, the rear sight and front sight are horizontally aligned, and point into the center of the target.

Illustration © Gila May-Hayes

the trigger and no anticipation of the shot are key components to effective trigger manipulation at any speed.

Make it a surprise

Why should I be surprised when the gun goes off? Obviously, if my finger's on the trigger, I should expect the gun to fire. The surprise I'm talking about is not being so focused on the act of pulling the trigger that I can predict that the gun is going to fire *at this exact instant*.

Again, why? Were you surprised by the noise and shock in your hand the first time you fired a handgun? I think we all were. Our bodies said, "That's horrible, let's find a way to avoid it next time." Even though our *minds* know we can survive this "adversive stimulus," the body will instinctively try to protect itself. If you know exactly when the gun is going to fire, your body will flinch as it tries to get away from the recoil and the noise. The flinch or jerking movement takes the gun off target and the bullet goes astray. *If you do not know when the gun is going to fire, you cannot flinch.* Make each shot a surprise.

Follow through

Like bowling or golf, follow through is important to accurate shot placement. Follow through with a firearm is the act of re-aligning the sights after the recoil of the shot, and centering them on the target for a follow up shot *before* releasing the trigger. Even if a second shot is not needed (in competition, for example) making a complete follow through keeps the shooter from raising her head to look at the target while firing the last shot. When the shooter peeks at the target, the sights are

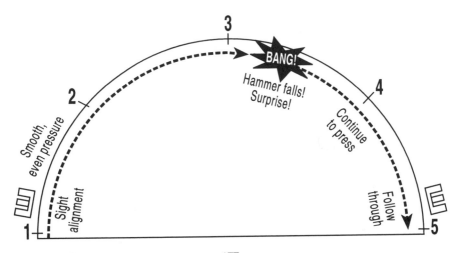

disturbed at the moment the gun fires, and the shot goes wild. In self defense, follow through prepares the handgun and the shooter to make a second shot if the threat is still active.

Grip

Still having some misses? Check your stance and your grip. Because a firearm recoils with each shot fired, a rock-firm grip is needed to maintain control and to aim the gun for consecutive shots. The dominant hand grasps the gun butt with the web pressed up against the grip tang at the top of the backstrap. Gripping the gun too low on the stocks allows the muzzle to rise unnecessarily during firing. Grip as high on the grips as you can for maximum control. The non-firing hand wraps completely around the firing hand. Fingers dovetail between the firing hand knuckles, and the non-firing hand's thumb sits right on top of the firing hand's thumbnail and locks down, pushing the thumbs against the gun.

Stance

A good shooting grip needs the support of strong footing, in the same way a house needs a good foundation to withstand wind storms. The Isosceles stance is the strongest and fastest to assume, based on shoulder-width feet, with arms locked straight out for fast, accurate firing.

A strong wrap-around grip demonstrated on the .40 caliber Glock 23.

The aggressive Isosceles stance is a fast and stable shooting posture.

The basis of your shooting stance is foot position. Feet must be placed an immodest shoulder width apart. Women students find this the most unnatural part of the training. They have excellent hand-eye coordination and can manipulate the little safety levers and magazine release buttons well, but standing with their legs wide is disconcerting. It feels *bad*. People trained in a martial art are comfortable in a wide stance. They know they're vulnerable to knock-down attacks if they keep their feet together. Check that the feet aren't aligned as if the shooter was walking a tightrope.

Going up from the feet, the leg on the firing hand side is positioned to the rear and is straight at the knee. The non-dominant leg is forward and can flex at the knee to act as a shock absorber against the gun's recoil. Don't lock both knees—that's inflexible and wobbly: under attack you need to be springy and resilient. The hips face the target straight on, with the hips and buttocks tucked forward. The shoulders likewise face the target squarely. Arms are locked straight out, punching the gun toward the target. The head may tuck down into the shoulders a little, a technique that combats high shots.

If the assailant runs away, but you aren't sure the entire area is safe, you'll want to get out of the area, gun in hand. The range ready position is very adaptable. Maintain your strong grip on the gun, tuck your elbows against your hips and move away. This keeps the gun out of reach of an assailant who may try to disarm you, while keeping it instantly ready to punch out into a shooting stance.

Dry fire

You don't need to go to the range to practice a smooth, controlled trigger pull, speed reloads, or draw and dry fire skills. Champion pistol shooters all practice dry fire. It is inexpensive: no ammunition needed; it is practical: you can safely do it almost anywhere. Best of all, it lets you ingrain a perfect trigger pull *without* the adversive stimuli of the gun firing, so it trains the body to pull the trigger smoothly without flinching.

Any gun handling demands total attention to safety. Bill Burris and Phil Shave of the Washington State Criminal Justice Training Commission teach a dry fire ritual that will keep you safe *if* adhered to with the same faithfulness that devout Catholics attend mass. The term *ritual* is used to remind you that this is a strict order of events which you must follow in this order, in the same way, every time you practice shooting techniques off the range.

DRY FIRE RITUAL

1. No distractions permitted. Send the children away, turn the phone recorder on and the TV and radio off!

2. Remove all ammunition and put it in a different room; allow no ammunition of any kind in the practice room.

3. Choose a safe aim point that is solid enough to stop bullets.

4. Mental shift to practice mode:

    Repeat out loud, so you can hear yourself make the statement, "This is practice. The gun is not loaded." Repeat it three times.

5. Perform dry fire practice or gun maintenance.

6. Mental shift back to reality mode.

    Repeat out loud and hear yourself say, "Practice is over. This is real. This gun is loaded." Make the statement aloud three times.

7. Put the gun away immediately and do not handle it for several hours.

Why does the ritual require audible, verbal declarations about the gun's status? Like computers, humans receive and process information from different "ports." The verbal statement that the gun is unloaded for dry fire practice gives you permission to pull the trigger. At the ritual's end, the mental acknowledgment that the gun is now loaded can be greatly emphasized by employing verbal and audible cues. Listen to yourself make the statement that the gun is loaded.

Finding a safe aim point in condominiums or apartments can be difficult. Remember, handgun bullets will penetrate sheet rock like it was butter, and will go through 2"x4"s, as well. If you have a basement, go down and aim at walls where concrete backed by dirt would catch a bullet. If you don't have a basement, consider a tightly packed bookcase (aim at the side so that two or three feet of books could stop a negligent discharge). We have a large steel gun safe we dry fire towards. The concrete wall or the gun safe, however, endangers the practicing shooter and others from ricochet, if a negligent round goes through the gun. In dry fire, obey the rule to remove *all* ammunition from the room. This includes "dummy" rounds used to simulate jam clearing. Dummy rounds have a mysterious way of migrating into real ammunition, and vice versa.

Dry firing—squeezing the trigger one or two hundred times—conditions the body to make one motion, squeezing the trigger. Muscle memory is stronger than mental determination. If you handle your loaded gun right after dry fire practice, your muscles are *conditioned* to squeeze the trigger. Put the gun away after dry fire practice.

Productive dry fire practice is more than just pulling the trigger a hundred times. Be completely focused on what is happening when you pull the trigger. Watch the front sight religiously. Does it move from side to side, does it dip during the trigger pull? The reason you are in the basement pulling the trigger on an empty gun is to learn to keep the front sight perfectly aligned in the rear sights during the entire trigger squeeze. If you do not concentrate on the task at hand your time is wasted and bad habits reinforced.

Having determined your safe aim point, mount a target at which you can aim. A white sheet of paper with a cross drawn on it is fine. Assume your Isosceles shooting stance, get a good grip on the gun and press the trigger smoothly. As an alternative exercise, balance a dime or penny

A coin balanced on the front sight reveals any jerking in the trigger pull during dryfire.

on the front sight, and press the trigger. If you have any gun motion during the trigger squeeze, the coin will fall, revealing that you jerked the trigger!

Speed reloads with the semi-auto are best practiced with the slide and barrel removed and magazines inserted only into the frame. Take the gun apart, then practice with loaded magazines over a bed or couch. The loaded magazines give you the same weight and feel of a real reload, while the disassembled gun removes the danger of practicing with live ammunition.

Never practice reloads during the same session you are practicing draw and fire routines or any other trigger action skill. The body performs the skills you teach it. As Massad Ayoob says: the moment your training succeeds, you will draw and negligently fire a round in the unsafe environment of your home.

Gun handling skills

After you have mastered basic sight picture, grip, and stance, you need to refine skills to keep the gun firing during combat or competition. Safe speed reloads are important, as is the ability to clear out any malfunction the weapon may experience.

You should have only one reload technique—a speed reload. Don't allow yourself to ingrain sloppy reloading habits while shooting for fun or during slow fire practice. The motions you make during fun and practice are the movements your body will make under stress.

Jim Cirillo, who survived a number of gunfights during his stint with the New York Stake Out Squad, relates a number of stories where police officers repeated gun handling sequences that had unintentionally been part of their training.

Some years ago, Cirillo relates, the officers were trained to shoot a course of fire then unload their empty brass cases into a can provided for that purpose. They were then to reload and shoot again. Reports from street encounters told of policemen who emptied their revolver at the assailant, turned and looked for the brass can *while the gunfight was still going on.* During a lethal encounter, the officers duplicated their range training, right down to the detail of looking for the brass case receptacle.

In an armed confrontation, the useless empties must be discarded as quickly as possible, new ammunition inserted and the gun brought back up on target in a matter of seconds. In the comfort of your living room, you may be tempted to say, "of course, I already knew that." But on the range, do you catch your revolver cases in your hand; do you carefully pluck out your $40 semi-auto magazine before it can fall to the ground and become scratched?

Every practice reload should be treated as if it was part of a life-threatening confrontation.

Practice routines

Just like your smooth trigger pull, clearing malfunctions is a muscle-memory skill. You can reinforce your speed and ability to clear malfunctions on the range using dummy cartridges. Produced by Precision Gun Specialties, the bright orange Saf-T-Trainer dummy rounds can be inserted in a magazine between live rounds to simulate a failure to fire. When the gun goes click instead of bang, the student performs a malfunction clearance drill. Load several magazines at random, mixing in three or four dummy rounds with the live ammunition. Have a friend load the magazines, or mix several magazines till you cannot anticipate what order the shots will come in. The element of surprise makes the training realistic. In addition to rapidly performing the clearance drill, watching your front sight during the malfunction will reveal flinching if you've anticipated the shot.

Malfunction drills are a valuable part of your practice. Second-level training, that which follows your introductory course work, should include this kind of instruction. Clearing malfunctions increases your understanding of how your gun works, and adds to your capability and handling skill with the weapon. Repeating clearance drills imprints the motions on your mind, and should the weapon malfunction during a class or a match, you will be gratified by an automatic response that puts your hands in motion to get the gun back in the game. More important, if the gun fails on the street, your rapid, trained response may save your life.

Live fire drills and skills

It feels great to reach the skill level where you can bring the gun up to the target and drill out an inch-or-two hole in the center. It is a great affirmation of your practice paying off in an important survival skill.

Now it is time for you to be sure you can perform that skill under life-or-death stress, on the move and on demand. Ask your instructors about intermediate and advanced training that teaches combat readiness. Courses you now need should include one-handed shooting, weak hand shooting, use of protective cover, low-light shooting, and realistic scenarios and role playing drills. Ask for training in using a quick or partial sight picture for fast, close-quarters shots. These are some of the abilities you need to add to your repertoire of survival skills.

When you go shooting with friends or practice alone, make the accuracy of each round fired of paramount importance. Don't train your body to shoot without a proper combat grip, stance, and sight alignment. If shooting with others, set up a friendly competition with some kinds of stakes. Every shot outside the X ring can "cost" a quarter's donation to the homeless people's fund or some other organization like your area's grass roots gun rights lobby. With shooters of varying skills, establish a handicap, like the more skilled shooter firing left handed, to make it truly competitive.

Games to induce the "rush"

A great way to stay in practice is to join a practical shooting league. The premier source for combat shooting competition is the International Practical Shooter's Confederation (IPSC). An IPSC match generally consists of five or six stages of fire with targets arranged to simulate armed assailants and innocent bystanders. A good stage will include targets that move or targets that drop when hit, sight line obstacles, use of cover or firing from a kneeling or prone position. It is excellent practice and always shows me areas where my skills need improvement.

When shooting competition one must remain aware that the match is a game, not realistic training for an actual armed encounter. Game rules often require the shooter to engage targets under conditions that would likely get you killed on the street. I like to remind myself "This is a game. I am here to practice drawing, reloading and shooting accurately. This is *not* tactical training."

Other competitive shooting events include bowling pin matches. It sounds a little weird, but shooting the wily bowling pin has become very popular since the mid-70s, when soft body armor inventor Richard Davis established the first big pin match. It is surprisingly practical. The bowling pin, at about 15 inches tall and three to four inches wide is very similar in size to the vital area on a human assailant we call the "center of mass." Bowling pins are reaction targets—when hit, they react. Well-aimed hits will push the pin off a table, sloppy hits will merely knock them over. You can learn a lot about precision shot placement by shooting bowling pins. Tables of five to eleven pins comprise the shooting "stages" in a bowling pin match, simulating multiple assailants. The shooter must follow the front sight from one pin to the next without looking up to see the results of their shooting.

Ask your local gun range about bowling pin matches as well as Police Pistol Competition (PPC) shooting. PPC uses unmoving paper targets, but requires accuracy and speed. All three are excellent places to test your skills against other shooters. Consider this: if in competition, you are the last to get your shot off, could you survive against an armed assailant on the street?

Speed and smoothness

Most shooting competition uses the shooter's time as part of the scoring formula, recognizing that the first bullet that hits a vital spot may win

The author shoots in the Second Chance Combat Shoot bowling pin match.

a street fight. You need to develop speed, but not at the expense of accuracy.

Speed is not a product of hurrying, it comes from eliminating all unnecessary motions in your shooting. It comes from *smoothness*.

IPSC competition is one of the author's favorite past times.

Never rush your movements to the point that they become jerky. The tension of hurrying will steal the smoothness that is the trademark of champion shooters.

20
Kids and Guns

Television is a powerful teacher. By the time they finish elementary school, American children have seen 8,000 murders and 100,000 acts of violence on television, according to the American Psychiatric Society. The only gun handling they have witnessed has been *draw, point, and shoot* in cartoons and by actors portraying criminals and police officers alike. Put a gun in the hand of a young viewer and the TV-trained response is to point the gun at a person and pull the trigger. They been taught this deadly response in their own living room, sometimes in the presence of their parents. TV has given guns an attractive mystique. Shown in the hands of the popular actors, they represent power, command respect, and are integral to the climax of the show. Is it any wonder that children want toy guns to play with? Is it any wonder that children sneak out their parents' guns when the parents are away, and experiment with holding and aiming (and sometimes tragically firing) these deadly weapons?

The Center for Disease Control reported that handgun and long gun accidents killed 34 children under age of 5 in 1984. The National Safety Council states that handgun accident fatalities took the lives of between 50 and 55 kids under the age of 15 in 1980.[1] Gun accidents are preventable. You can keep your children *out* of these statistics.

Gun myths claim that children can't pull a heavy double action revolver trigger or rack the slide of a semi-auto to get a cartridge into the chamber. That may be true under "test" circumstances, but children are cunning and will figure out how to use leverage, pushing the slide against another object, pulling that heavy trigger with both fingers, and other yet-unthought-of ways to load and fire the weapon. The same principle applies to safe boxes that use sequenced buttons and other gimmicks to secure the gun.

Hiding the gun is absolutely ineffective. As a child, didn't you find where your parents hid your birthday or Christmas present at least once, probably repeatedly? A locking safe or safe box with key is about the only effective "hiding" place. Keys must stay on the parent's person, however, not left where the child can pick up and use them.

Gun owners have a responsibility to keep their guns secure from unauthorized hands, but parents must prepare their children for the day they find an unsupervised gun in someone else's home.

During the fall of 1993 I appeared on a talk show as part of a panel that included a woman whose adolescent son had been killed by another boy playing with his parents' guns. Let me tell you that this kind of gun irresponsibility gives the gun control lobby the strongest argument possible. No one will take to task a grieving mother. If you are unwilling to keep your guns locked away and secured from unauthorized hands, I believe you are jeopardizing the gun rights of responsible, careful gun owners.

Dispel the myth

The first chore is to remove the firearm's attraction. Tell your children a gun is an emergency rescue tool, much like the fire extinguisher or rope and ladder used to save lives during a house fire. When TV or a film shows gun use, discuss it with your children. If the portrayal was inaccurate, for example, if a gun-wounded hero appears the same evening with just a bandage over a shoulder wound, explain to your children that in real life that person would be (a) dead (b) unable to use the arm (c) hospitalized for a lengthy period, but definitely not back on patrol! Explain that death is a very real possibility when a firearm is used. A gun's impact can be demonstrated in safe live fire at an outdoor shooting range. Fire into melons or water jugs to illustrate a bullet's destructive power. While actual ballistics are different, this is an impressive way to introduce young children to the handgun's purpose: destruction.

Repression has never decreased attraction. Your child's fascination with guns will only increase when you tell him or her that guns are "just for adults" and that they must never, never touch one. Children crave adult experiences. Find safe, appropriate ways to give your kids responsible involvement with your firearms. Your child's first hands-on experience with your guns can be during cleaning. Make the weapon safe: put all ammunition in a separate room, then invite the child to help you clean the gun.

Show the child how the gun works, and how to check that the gun is empty, emphasizing the first two rules of safe gun handling:

Treat every gun as if it is loaded.
Never point a gun at anything you are not willing to shoot.

Your example is the most effective teacher. Enforce safe muzzle direction, do not allow the gun to "sweep" family members while you prepare to clean it. Decide what "help" the child can offer: perhaps by cleaning semi-auto's feed ramp or scrubbing the front of the revolver's cylinder with a nylon toothbrush. Older kids can "detail" the crevices and small recesses with cotton swabs.

Having taught the children to treat every firearm as if it is loaded, instruct them to leave any gun where they find it and get an adult to secure it. It may be appropriate to let your children know you will reward their safe behavior if they leave any place a gun is brought out without your express approval. Do not try to teach them to unload guns. The potential for disaster is too great.

Should children shoot?

Children of shooters will probably want to go to the range with their parents and will soon ask to fire the guns. Under direct parental supervision, the child may be allowed to first watch and hear the guns being fired. When the noise ceases to bother them, the child and parent may hold and fire a .22 rifle. I prefer the rifle to small caliber handguns because the long barrel makes it easier to enforce safe muzzle direction. The rifle is easier to aim and shoot accurately, so the child's experience is positive.

Now, on the range, begin drilling the other rules of safe gun handling. Explain the reasons for these rules and be sure they are obeyed all the time.

Keep your finger off the trigger until the gun sights are on target.
Be sure of your target and what is behind it.

Not until the child has attained the maturity to assume personal responsibility and to understand *what death means* should they be allowed to handle firearms without the parent in direct contact. The age will vary from child to child. A gauge of a child's understanding can be something as simple as their safe behavior as pedestrians or with bicycles on the street in front of your home. A careless or risk-taking youngster has no place on a firing range—wait a year or so until they have matured a little. If, however, your child demonstrates an understanding of life and death on the street, you can use that metaphor to be sure they understand the lethality of careless gun handling.

The NRA's Eddie Eagle program for young children teaches safe gun handling.[2] Some NRA gun ranges have junior leagues that let the children compete in a well-supervised atmosphere. State fish and game departments usually sponsor hunter education classes that are good resources for gun safety instruction. If your children are extremely interested in your guns, offer to enroll them in an organized youth shooting program. Attend or volunteer to help with the classes to be sure the gun-handling is safe.

As your children demonstrate that they understand life and death, and the handgun's potential for tragedy, let them know that you will happily take them shooting when they ask and when practical. Their half of the agreement is a solemn pledge never to touch a gun without your presence or your permission. The offer can extend to friends with parental permission, giving your child the ability to walk away from an

A .22 rimfire rifle is a good "starter" gun for a child.

unsupervised gun saying, "That's no big deal. My mom and dad take me shooting when I ask. If you put that gun down, I'll ask them if you can come along next weekend." If the offer fails, your child *must* walk away, but can do so with the prestige that they are allowed to use guns responsibly.

Younger children can begin their safe-gun attitudes with their toy guns. Use these toys as training devices to teach the four prime gun handling rules. Never allow your kids to point gun replicas at family members. A lot of us have grave reservations about even allowing toy guns in the home, but gun use is so integral to American culture that children denied toy guns will adopt other objects to substitute as guns in their play. I think it is more realistic to allow a toy phaser that bears little resemblance to an actual firearm and use that toy as a training device.

Living with guns and children

If you bought your gun for personal and home defense, you need ways to keep that gun accessible for emergency use while keeping it out of reach of your children. The solution is to keep the gun holstered on the

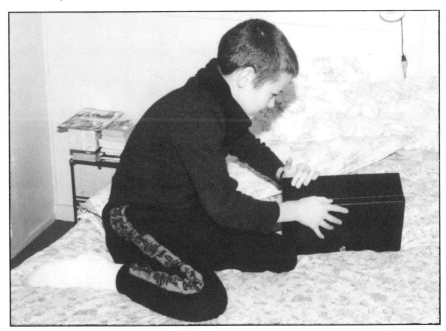

A locking gun box like the SafeGard™ Gun Vault sold by Aspen Outdoors, is an inexpensive alternative to a full-sized safe, and keeps one or two personal handguns out of the hands of children.

parent's body at all times, then locked in a bed-side drawer at night. Realistically, wearing a gun is probably not comfortable enough to continue inside the safe confines of your home. If the parent takes the gun off before bedtime, it must be secured in a locked box or gun safe *immediately*, not put atop the refrigerator or in a dresser drawer.

One of the fastest lock boxes we've found is the SafeGard™ Gun Vault.[3] The latches are concealed in two of four buttons that look like "feet" on the bottom of the box. To unlock the box, the adult presses the appropriate "feet" and the lid pops open. It takes quite a bit of coordination and strength to push the feet in the right directions, so *young* children should not be able to access the gun. I wouldn't be inclined to trust it too much, though. Kids are cunning and every parent can relate an amazing tale of kids getting into child-proof bottles or defeating other safety devices. The SafeGard™ box, however, is good as a night-time repository.

A genuine safe, whether big or small, is the best place to leave your guns when you're out of the house. The best safes have dials and keys, doubly protecting the contents. If a parent is concerned that an unruly adolescent might have figured out the safe combination, the key lock adds an extra ring of safety.

Your kids reflect your attitudes

Your responsible behavior with the gun will be reflected in your child's actions. Parents who respect the deadly power of their gun will safeguard their children until they are sure that firearms responsibility is understood. The best argument made for disarming the American public is a tragic shooting by a child misusing the parent's gun. If you bring a gun into your home, *please* have the responsibility and maturity to keep it in your hands only. If you do not think you can keep your gun out of your children's hands, consider a less deadly means of protection: oleoresin capsicum spray or large, mean dogs that love only your family. You must not endanger your children, yourself, and others by owning a gun without respecting its power.

[1] Data edited by Don B. Kates, *Guns, Murder and the Constitution*, 1991.

[2] National Rifle Association, 1600 Rhode Island Ave., N.W., Washington, DC 20036.

[3] Aspen Outdoors, source for the SafeGard™ Gun Vault, 1059 W. Market St., York, PA 17404, (800) 677-7747.

20
Etiquette for the Armed Civilian

The armed gang activity prevalent today has falsified the saying "an armed society is a polite society." Among legitimate gun owners, however, the statement remains true. As you adopt the self-reliant life style of one who is truly able to care for herself, you'll realize the responsibility that your self-reliance carries.

Preparation and foresight are elements of the gun owner's life. Foresight means that we live our lives in such a way that our actions and activities don't demonstrate careless disregard for human life. Simple things like the jokes we tell or the t-shirt slogans on our backs can come back to haunt us in a courtroom.

T-shirt slogans that indicate disregard for life or the lawful use of guns give a message that you don't intend to use your firearm in a judicious manner. Not only can this message be used by prosecution following a self defense shooting; it also fuels the anti-gun forces that threaten our right to use deadly force in self defense.

Avoid intemperate remarks *before* to any self defense actions. Jokes and remarks about news stories like "*I* would have killed that bastard," can surface in court as evidence that you wanted to kill someone.

A joke about telling someone to "make my day" may pop up if you ever have to face a violent assailant. Not only can such comments fuel your assailant's rage, they can come back to harm your legal defense if overhead by witnesses. "If you're judicious in your day-to-day comments, hard-to-defend phrases probably won't pop up under stress," advises Evan Marshall.

Keep it a secret
We talked earlier about keeping the gun out of sight, not showing it off to visitors in your home. When carrying a gun for self defense you must

be even more discrete. It is foolish to allow the gun or its outline to show in public. Moreover, in most jurisdictions, it is illegal to reveal the presence of your gun. Allowing the gun to show is considered threatening behavior, and often violates laws that give people the right not to feel endangered by the presence of guns.

Beyond the law, it is unwise and risky to reveal that you are armed. In some, you may bring up harsh anti-gun sentiments, but others may see it as an opportunity to try to take it from you.

The gun must not be drawn and pointed unless you believe you are in immediate and unavoidable danger of death or grave bodily harm. If you cannot justify your actions by these criteria, leave the gun in its holster and get away from the perceived threat. The gun is not for warning. If you present it, you must have justification for its use, for by pointing a gun at another person, you have put them in fear of death.

Have a plan

Preparation means knowing what to do if assaulted. Decide how you will respond to a variety of circumstances: a break-in at your home, an assault against you in your home, an assault against another family member, an assault in your car or on the street. Keep the plan private, "that's between you and your God," Marshall comments. Think through your responses to various scenarios. If you realize you don't know what to do, seek out further training.

Merely owning a gun for self defense is not enough. The owner must become and remain skilled in its proper use and knowledgeable about when it may be used. The government and news media campaign against sensible people who own guns to provide for their own defense makes it crucial that our use of the gun is only when no other avenue of escape or deflection exists.

Taking responsibility

When an innocent person uses a gun in self defense, the news media gives scant mention or ignores the value the gun held for the survivor in their moment of danger. We live in a society that does not understand the awful, yet sometimes necessary, act of using a gun in self defense. Every use of the gun is portrayed as criminal, bloodthirsty and indefensible. The rights of criminals sometimes receive more attention than the rights of victims and the future victims the offender will assault.

Clearly the agony of the victims is not of sufficient importance to convince our leaders that violent offenders must be imprisoned permanently. So long as these abusers are set free to prey on the helpless, the numbers of atrocious attacks will increase. So long as movies and television instruct the impressionable in rape, murder and violence, women will be targeted as victims of men without consciences. Until a majority of women say "Enough!" and assume the responsibility of using deadly force in self defense, we *will* continue to be victims.

For some, the gun will never be acceptable. These women must exercise a much higher level of prudence about their surroundings. Intermediate weapons like pepper sprays, the Persuader, and empty hand defenses are useful, and a high level of training and proficiency will be crucial.

Each individual woman needs to decide how she will protect herself and her family. Our right, and the right of our children, to survive unmolested, is worth protecting passionately. It is worth the time and expense of training and the cost of the tools—whether that be a gun or another weapon. It is worth the time needed to wrestle with the question "could I kill in self defense?" And it is worth the effort to develop realistic self defense plans we are capable of executing.

Stay alert and aware; stay alive. Be safe.

Training with the author

If you are interested in hosting
a training course taught by
Gila May-Hayes, or would
like information on how
to attend one of her
courses in the Seattle
area, please call or write:

The Firearms Academy of Seattle, Inc.

P.O. Box 2814, Kirkland, WA 98083
(800) 327-2666

Courses available include:

Introduction to Handguns

Advanced Handgun Skills

Persuader Certification

Pepper Spray Certification

Weapon Retention and Disarming

If you enjoyed Effective Defense...

you will also like reading and studying the following books, which are either mentioned in the text, or recommended by the author in her training courses.

In the Gravest Extreme $9.95
The Role of the Firearm in Personal Protection, by Massad F. Ayoob

StressFire $9.95
by Massad F. Ayoob

StressFire II, Advanced Combat Shotgun $9.95
by Massad F. Ayoob

The Semi-Automatic Pistol in Police Service and Self Defense..$9.95
by Massad F. Ayoob

The Street Smart Gun Book $11.95
by John S Farnam

Armed and Female $4.50
by Paxton Quigley

Handgun Stopping Power, The Definitive Study $39.95
by Evan Marshall and Edwin Sanow

The Professional's Guide to Handgun Cleaning...........................$6.95
by Marty Hayes

To order any of the above books, send check or money order for the full amount, plus $3.00 shipping costs (Washington State residents also add 8.2% sales tax) to:

FAS Books

P.O. Box 2814, Kirkland, WA 98083
You may also order with a VISA or MasterCard by calling (800) 327-2666